NEW DIRECTIONS FOR MENTAL HEALTH SERVICES

H. Richard Lamb, *University of Southern California*
EDITOR-IN-CHIEF

Neurobiological Disorders in Children and Adolescents

Enid Peschel
Yale University School of Medicine

Richard Peschel
Yale University School of Medicine

Carol W. Howe
National Alliance for the Mentally Ill

James W. Howe
National Alliance for the Mentally Ill

EDITORS

Number 54, Summer 1992

JOSSEY-BASS PUBLISHERS
San Francisco

NEUROBIOLOGICAL DISORDERS IN CHILDREN AND ADOLESCENTS
Enid Peschel, Richard Peschel, Carol W. Howe, James W. Howe (eds.)
New Directions for Mental Health Services, no. 54
H. Richard Lamb, Editor-in-Chief

Microfilm copies of issues and articles are available in 16mm and 35mm, as well as microfiche in 105mm, through University Microfilms Inc., 300 North Zeeb Road, Ann Arbor, Michigan 48106.

LC 87-646993   ISSN 0193-9416   ISBN 1-55542-758-8

NEW DIRECTIONS FOR MENTAL HEALTH SERVICES is part of The Jossey-Bass Social and Behavioral Sciences Series and is published quarterly by Jossey-Bass Inc., Publishers, 350 Sansome Street, San Francisco, California 94104-1310 (publication number USPS 493-910). Second-class postage paid at San Francisco, California, and at additional mailing offices. POSTMASTER: Send address changes to New Directions for Mental Health Services, Jossey-Bass Inc., Publishers, 350 Sansome Street, San Francisco, California 94104-1310.

SUBSCRIPTIONS for 1992 cost $52.00 for individuals and $70.00 for institutions, agencies, and libraries.

EDITORIAL CORRESPONDENCE should be sent to the Editor-in-Chief, H. Richard Lamb, Department of Psychiatry and the Behavioral Sciences, U.S.C. School of Medicine, 1934 Hospital Place, Los Angeles, California 90033.

Cover photograph by Wernher Krutein/PHOTOVAULT © 1990.

 The paper used in this journal is acid-free and meets the strictest guidelines in the United States for recycled paper (50 percent recycled waste, including 10 percent post-consumer waste). Manufactured in the United States of America.

CONTENTS

PART Two: Future Directions for Society Based on the
Neurobiological Revolution

EDITORS' NOTES

In the past ten to fifteen years, a revolution has occurred in molecular biology and neurobiology. This revolution has profoundly changed our understanding of severe mental illness. For the first time ever, consistent and reproducible neuroanatomical and neurochemical abnormalities are being documented that are directly correlated with various forms of clinically severe "mental" illness in children and adolescents. The list of severe "mental" illnesses in children and adolescents that are characterized by neurochemical malfunctions or neuroanatomical malformations in the brain or both includes autism and pervasive developmental disorders, obsessive-compulsive disorder, Tourette's syndrome, bipolar and major depressive disorders, attention deficit hyperactivity disorder, anxiety disorders, and schizophrenia. Because of the irrefutable scientific evidence that is being accumulated, we have used the term *neurobiological disorder (NBD)* to describe these severe, chronic "mental" illnesses that have a physical, neurochemical, or neuroanatomical basis. Because of the incidence, severity, and chronicity of these neurobiological disorders, these NBD represent a greater public health problem than either childhood leukemia or all childhood cancers combined.

The purpose of this volume is twofold. First, it summarizes the latest scientific findings as they relate to NBD in children and adolescents. Second, it recommends fundamental changes in our society's institutions—including the medical profession, the insurance industry, the educational system, and the legal system. These changes must occur as a direct result of the new scientific understanding of NBD.

This volume emphasizes the discoveries of the neuroscience revolution during the past few years. Consequently, it stresses the latest scientific data about NBD in children and adolescents and deemphasizes opinion, theory, and belief systems that had evolved over the years but that were based on little or no scientific evidence. This contribution is very much needed and long overdue. It will be a most helpful volume for all caring professionals, caring families, and the caring public.

There are two major sections to this volume. Part One, "The Biological Basis of Neurobiological Disorders in Children and Adolescents," contains thirteen chapters written by some of the leading neuroscience researchers in child and adolescent psychiatry in the United States. Chapter One (Ciaranello) provides a concise summary of brain development and its possible relationship with autism and pervasive developmental disorders. Chapter Two (Courchesne) presents additional scientific data about childhood autism. Chapters Three (Rapoport) and Four (Leckman) are devoted to the neurobiological basis of two quintessential models for NBD, obsessive-compulsive disorder and Tourette's syndrome, respectively. Chapters Five (Strober) and Six (Brent) document the decisive scientific evidence for the underlying genetic and neurochemical components of both bipolar disorder and major depressive disorder. Chapter Seven (Amaya-Jackson, Mesco, McGough, and Cantwell) discusses the neurobiological and genetic basis, as well as the treatment, of the most commonly diagnosed behavioral disorder in childhood, attention deficit hyperactivity disorder (ADHD). While Chapter Eight (Elia, Stoff, and Coccaro) explains how a group of impulsive disruptive behavioral disorders (conduct disorder, ADHD, and borderline personality disorder) may share common clinical and biological characteristics, Chapter Nine (Rifkin) addresses the pharmacological treatment of conduct disorder, one of the most common disorders in children and adolescents. Chapter Ten (Black), which documents the strong hereditary-biological component in anxiety disorders, also demonstrates important relationships between anxiety disorders and depression. Chapter Eleven (Gordon) considers childhood schizophrenia, and Chapter Twelve (Weinberger) reviews modern neuroimaging techniques that have revolutionized the scientific study of NBD. Chapter Thirteen (Jensen), the concluding chapter of Part One, sets forth future directions for neuroscience research in children and adolescents.

Starting from the scientific foundation of Part One, Part Two, "Future Directions for Society Based on the Neurobiological Revolution," contains seven chapters. These address some of the ways in which the institutions of our society must translate the findings of the neurobiological revolution into reality-based actions to help children and adolescents severely disabled by their NBD. Chapter Fourteen (Peschel and Peschel) recommends that the medical, educational, governmental, legal, and social institutions of our society accept the scientific facts about NBD and integrate that scientific knowledge into reality-based programs, policies, and actions. Chapter Fifteen (VanDenBerg) delineates the successful, cost-effective "wrap-around" services program that benefited children and youth with NBD in the Alaska Youth Initiative. Chapters Sixteen (O'Keefe) and Seventeen (Spears) argue the crucial issue of obtaining insurance coverage for the physical-medical disorders called NBD on a par with other physical illnesses. Chapter Eighteen (Ervin) exposes the issue of parents who have been forced to relinquish custody of their child who is severely ill with NBD to obtain appropriate medical care. Chapter Nineteen (Sussan) addresses the special education requirements mandated by federal law for children with NBD. Finally, Chapter Twenty (McLoughlin) emphasizes that the focus of nonpharmacological treatment for children with NBD by the health care industry should be on supportive caring for the ill child and for the caring family.

In summary, NBD in children and adolescents must be addressed in terms of its underlying neurobiology and neuroanatomy. The question is no longer whether these serious chronic brain disorders have a biological basis in children and adolescents. The important questions now are the following: (1) What are the specific neurobiological abnormalities that characterize each NBD? and (2) How can we devise better medical treatments and services for all children severely ill with NBD? It is our profound hope that this book will represent only the initial attempt to grapple with these questions.

Enid Peschel
Richard Peschel
Carol W. Howe
James W. Howe
Editors

ENID PESCHEL is co-director of the Program for Humanities in Medicine and assistant professor (adjunct) of internal medicine at Yale University School of Medicine.

RICHARD PESCHEL is professor of therapeutic radiology at Yale University School of Medicine.

CAROL W. HOWE is membership chair of the National Alliance for the Mentally Ill Children and Adolescents Network (NAMI CAN) Advisory Council, Arlington, Virginia.

JAMES W. HOWE, an economist, was president of the National Alliance for the Mentally Ill (NAMI), Arlington, Virginia, from 1984 to 1986.

INTRODUCTION

The publication of this volume provides convincing evidence that psychiatry—accompanied by its two traveling companions, neuroscience and neuropharmacology—has returned from its self-imposed exile into the mainstream of medicine and biology. In two short decades, advances in neurobiology and genetics, assisted by novel imaging techniques, have dramatically changed the ecology of psychiatric research and of patient care. Now, new scientific findings, the products of laboratory experiments and controlled clinical trials, have replaced the prophetic, nonscientific pronouncements of the past that senior mentors had enunciated with great conviction. Gone, too, are the days when responsibility for the patient's illness could be deposited on the family's doorstep with impunity. The "who done it" approach has been dislodged by careful studies on genetic vulnerability and investigations designed to reveal the biological mechanisms by which stresses and other environmental insults affect the developing organism in general, and the central nervous system in particular. Today, physicians and other health professionals view family members as allies who can become effective partners in the treatment team only if they have been thoroughly educated about the patient's illness. Psychological management of patients has changed profoundly as well. The primary goal now is to assist in patients' rehabilitation by improving their coping skills. The pragmatic, cognitive approach replaces long-held and vague romantic notions that recovery can only take place through resolving conflicts.

Inevitably, the dizzying pace with which new information is being generated may give rise to premature speculations about the etiology and pathogenesis of psychiatric disorders, as well as overstated declarations about the effectiveness of some treatments. It is most encouraging to note, therefore, that the scientists who have contributed to this volume fully expect and, indeed, hope that once biological markers are identified, these preliminary hypotheses will be revised or altogether abandoned and that the descriptive diagnosis system currently in use will undergo substantial changes.

The editors of this volume have ensured that professional and lay readers will receive a balanced and critical update on new developments. I hope that the success of this publication will encourage them to continue to provide this valuable public service in the coming years.

Thomas Detre

THOMAS DETRE is senior vice president of health sciences and president of the Medical and Health Care Division at the University of Pittsburgh.

PART ONE:

The Biological Basis of
Neurobiological Disorders
in Children and Adolescents

Normal brain development involves a series of exquisitely complex and highly orchestrated events; disruptions in normal brain development provide a useful model for understanding infantile autism and other pervasive developmental disorders.

Brain Development: Pervasive Developmental Disorders and Infantile Autism

Roland D. Ciaranello

Pervasive developmental disorders (PDD) constitute a group of disorders that are evident in infancy, childhood, or adolescence and that are characterized by severe impairments in many basic areas of psychological development. These areas include reciprocal social interactions, communication skills, and imaginative activities. A restricted repertoire of activities and interests is also common. According to the DSM-III-R (American Psychiatric Association, 1987), a variety of diagnostic terms have been used in the past to describe PDD, including atypical development, symbiotic psychosis, childhood psychosis, and childhood schizophrenia. Within the PDD classification, there is only one consistent and generally recognizable subtype, infantile autism, which can be defined according to a number of specific criteria.

Patients with PDD who do not meet the specific criteria of infantile autism are classified as Pervasive Developmental Disorder Not Otherwise Specified (PDDNOS). Because PDDNOS applies to such a wide spectrum of disorders that vary greatly in severity and expression, the designation PDDNOS is more descriptive than diagnostic. As a result, scientific research into the underlying etiology, neuroanatomy, neurobiology, and genetics of PDDNOS has been severely limited. Until more specific and consistently

Studies described from the author's laboratory were funded by a program-project grant from the NIMH (MH 39437), the Spunk Fund, the Rebecca & Solomon Baker Fund, and the endowment to the Nancy Pritzker Laboratory.

identifiable subtypes are defined, a systematic study of PDDNOS will remain problematical. However, infantile autism serves as a useful model for all PDD, and it is reasonable to assume that most of the conceptual framework and scientific knowledge developed about infantile autism will also apply to patients with PDDNOS. Because infantile autism can be consistently diagnosed according to a set of specific criteria, it is more amenable to scientific research and study.

Two facts about PDD are clear: (1) It is a lifelong, chronic disorder that generally involves such severe social impairments that independent living is not possible. (2) Based on its chronicity, severity, and incidence (there are 1 to 1.5 cases per 1,000 people), *PDD represents a greater public health problem than either childhood leukemia or other childhood cancers.*

The rest of this chapter focuses on the most clearly defined subtype of PDD, infantile autism, and on normal brain development. However, it must be emphasized that much of what follows also applies to PDDNOS.

Infantile Autism

Infantile autism is a severe disturbance in brain development that results in a distinct cluster of neurological and behavioral disturbances, including extreme social withdrawal, persistent preoccupation with parts of objects, ritualistic behaviors, motor stereotypies, and failure to develop normal language. Once present, autism typically affects the person for life, although treatment and intervention strategies can do a lot to ameliorate the severity of the disorder.

Much more common than childhood leukemia, autism occurs more frequently than all forms of childhood cancer combined. Because it is a chronic, lifelong disorder, the social cost of autism, measured in the need for special services—education, respite care, and the drain on family resources—is enormous. Yet the research dollars allocated to finding autism's causes and treatments are a trivial fraction of those spent on other childhood diseases.

A number of factors are known to cause autism. The best studied is viral infection with rubella virus or cytomegalovirus during pregnancy. While these infections are quite mild in their effect on the mother, they are devastating to the developing fetus and are associated with a wide variety of birth defects, as well as with fetal death. Many metabolic diseases are also associated with autism. In metabolic diseases, chemicals needed for normal body function cannot be made, while many unneeded chemicals build up in excess, becoming toxic. Mental retardation is a common occurrence in metabolic disease; autism is seen much less frequently. Phenylketonuria, tuberous sclerosis, and adenylosuccinate lyase deficiency are all examples of metabolic diseases in which autism is sometimes seen.

For the vast majority of cases, the cause of autism is unknown. But the fact that autism occurs in conjunction with other diseases that disrupt brain development has led researchers to propose that autism also arises from disruptions in brain development. This hypothesis states that instead of being caused by a virus or an impaired chemical reaction, autism occurs when something interferes with the normal pattern of brain development. This may either take the form of outside events (such as viral infection or brain trauma) or may happen through processes intrinsic to the developing brain.

Brain Development

The development of the human brain is an exquisitely complex, highly orchestrated event that begins shortly after conception and is not completed until the seventh or eighth year of life. During early brain development, brain cells are born, move to take up their positions to form the brain's delicate structures, and then establish the connections with other brain nerve cells that are at the heart of the brain's information processing function. These processes take place in definite stages during brain development, but their temporal boundaries cannot be specified with precision. The brain is not a homogeneous entity; rather, it is subdivided into many different structures that carry out diverse, distinct tasks. Each behaves almost as a separate organ, obeying its own developmental timetable. With this in mind, we recognize four critical stages: neurulation, histogenesis, cell migration, and neuritic differentiation. Disruptions in any of these four stages can lead to disturbances in brain functioning, varying from very subtle to devastating. In general, the earlier in development something goes wrong, the more severe its consequences.

Neurulation. Neurulation, the first step in brain development, begins around day 18 of gestation and is complete around the sixth week. The entire nervous system starts life as a flat plate of cells that begins to fold up to form a closed (neural) tube by day 21. The front part of the tube will form the brain; the tube's back part will form the spinal cord. Nerve cells within the neural tube are now being born; these will ultimately give rise to all the brain's neurons.

Around day 28, the neural tube begins to undergo a series of swellings and contractions that change its shape from a simple tube to a configuration more closely resembling the brain and the spinal cord. At the front end, the brain begins to expand greatly in size, giving rise to what will become the cerebral cortex, cerebellum, and other structures.

Histogenesis. While the neural tube is growing and changing shape, cells within it are dividing and beginning their migrations. The primitive cells that had constituted the flat plate before the neural tube formed will give rise to three major cell types: *neurons* (nerve cells), *glia* (supporting cells), and *ependymal cells,* which line the cavities (ventricles) of the brain.

Around the sixth week of gestation, the first cerebral cortical neurons appear. As befits the most complex structure in the body, the final anatomy of the brain's cortex will not be completed until shortly before birth, and its "fine-tuning" will go on until well into childhood.

Migration. As cells are being born, they begin to migrate from the ventricular zone (in the brain's ventricles), where they arise, to the brain's outer layers. In this fascinating process, radial glia cells form "guide wires" along which cortical neurons migrate in a sequential process: they attach themselves, pull up, let go, and reattach. Equally fascinating is the fact that the cortex develops "inside out." The earliest-born neurons travel the shortest distance from the ventricular zone, while the last-born neurons travel the farthest, to the top layers of the cortex.

Differentiation. Once neurons reach their destination in the brain, they undergo the last—and most complicated—stage in development: the formation of synaptic contacts. The brain's business is information processing: receiving stimuli, transferring information, communicating with all parts of the body, receiving information, and sending commands. This is done by the formation of synapses—regions where one nerve cell lies close to another but does not touch it. Across this infinitesimally small gap, neurotransmitters (chemicals) are released from one nerve, where they stimulate their neighboring nerve cells. Nerve cells receive information from thousands of surrounding cells by elaborating a complex, antenna-like structure called the *dendritic tree* that resembles a tree's branches. Each branch of the dendritic tree receives input from neighboring neurons. Information flows into the nerve cell down the dendritic branches, is processed by the cell body, and is converted into an electrical output. This output leaves the cell via a single axon, a long snake-like structure that liberates neurotransmitters from its end; these neurotransmitters then stimulate neighboring nerve cells.

The process of synapse formation is known as *neuritic differentiation*. When this process is complete, nerves will have established circuits and networks with their neighbors, as well as across long distances, thereby binding every part of the nervous system in a network of sublime complexity. The entire process is controlled by the genes that came together in the union of sperm and egg. Throughout, genes have issued the tiny chemical signals instructing the birth of cells, their spatial arrangements and re-arrangements, their migration, and their establishment of connectivity. Genes govern these processes by means of the information encoded in them and in response to incoming cues from the environment. Thus, the entire process of development depends on the proper interactions, over an extended time, between an organism's genes and the environment in which that organism is developing.

Given the extraordinary complexity of the brain and the millions upon millions of signals that must be processed during its development, we must wonder not just why the process goes wrong on occasion, but marvel how it goes right most of the time!

Autism and Genetics

There is abundant evidence that autism represents a failure—probably a relatively subtle one—in brain development. We might wonder at how a disorder as clinically consequential as autism could warrant the term *subtle,* but in terms of neuropathology, the description is accurate. Autopsies of brains of autistic individuals dying of other causes have failed to show evidence of structural brain abnormalities that could be consistently observed by large numbers of researchers. There have been intriguing reports of disruptions in the normal cellular patterns of isolated areas in the brain—in the cerebellum and hippocampus, for example—but nothing has been found to consistently implicate one brain area or one cellular abnormality. In most cases, the brains of autistic children look normal under the microscope.

How can we reconcile this? On the one hand, we have a neurodevelopmental disorder leading to profound clinical dysfunction; on the other, a brain that, with our current tools at least, looks perfectly normal. There are probably many answers, but I would offer this: (1) We probably do not have the right tools to see what we are looking for. (2) We do not really know what we are looking for. My view is that we are looking for a disturbance in connectivity between cells, where neurons have failed to make the right connections or have made the wrong ones. Unless we know exactly what to look for and where, we would never find so subtle a defect. If we had some idea where an anatomical defect might reside, we could probably utilize current methodologies to visualize it; for example, the electron microscope would easily reveal failures in synaptogenesis (the formation of synapses). But current techniques for examining synapses require precise knowledge of their location. We need a technique that scans the brain at the ultramicroscopic level, looking for disruptions in connectivity.

We do know that two lines of evidence implicate genes in the pathology of autism: (1) The entire process of brain development is orchestrated by genes. Without their precise function, brain development will not occur normally. (2) There is increasing clinical evidence that, in some families at least, autism is an inherited disorder. This evidence comes from two sources. Studies using identical twins who share identical genes show that when one twin is autistic, the other is autistic as often as 90 percent of the time. Also, studies have clearly indicated a genetic base for autism in families where more than one member is autistic.

Current research is aimed at finding the gene(s) involved in autism. While this promises to be an extremely difficult task, modern molecular genetic strategies offer great hope that the search will ultimately be successful. Already these strategies have led to the discovery of genes, previously unknown, for muscular dystrophy, cystic fibrosis, and neurofibromatosis.

Although there is great excitement in searching for a gene involved in autism, we must be sobered by the realization that even if such a gene is found, it is not likely to tell us everything we want to know about the disorder. There are several reasons for this: (1) Not all cases of autism are genetic. Indeed, the majority of cases probably arise from nongenetic causes such as viral infections, brain damage, or birth trauma. Therefore, finding a gene will tell us some very important things about autism, but not everything. (2) The genetics of autism are not at all straightforward. In our research, autism appears to be inherited as an autosomal dominant trait with incomplete penetrance, meaning that not everyone who should have the disorder exhibits it. At present, we cannot explain how two apparently normal parents can produce two or three autistic children. Nor can we explain why autistic boys outnumber girls by more than four to one. Other mysteries include the following: What keeps the autism gene(s) in the population, given that autistic individuals rarely marry or produce children? Are there mild forms of autism that might escape detection that could explain why the disorder appears to skip generations?

Our research indicates that there are mild forms of autism that do not prevent individuals from functioning in society, marrying, and having children. Such persons may have been called *high-functioning* autistics in childhood, or they may have been labeled *schizoid*. Our work indicates that some parents of families with several autistic children exhibit some signs of autism themselves and thus may be mildly affected. If this is true, it would explain why autism gene(s) remain in the population; it may provide answers to some of the other questions as well.

Treatment of Autism

The first step in providing effective treatment is an improved method of diagnosing autism early. This is important because the brain is very immature at birth: treatment interventions to foster acquisition of social, cognitive, and language skills might be much more effective if started at age twelve months than at age five. Yet most clinicians are uncomfortable making a diagnosis of autism before three or four years of age.

In the absence of distinct biological markers (chemical tests, reproducible measurements), the diagnosis of autism remains subjective and thus may vary widely among clinicians. Because early recognition of autism might lead to more effective therapies (due to the immature brain's plasticity, mentioned above), a major priority should be developing tools that lead to identifying autism in infants or very young children. Gene markers or, better yet, tests based on identification of abnormal gene products could recognize autism in utero and thus should lead to much earlier recognition of the disorder.

In the meantime, effective treatments for some of autism's symptoms are available. Flexible behavior modification strategies are effective in alleviating some of the disruptive behaviors. Language therapies have enabled many autistic children to communicate more effectively. Medications are available to help control some of the outburst behaviors, but these drugs have powerful side effects and should be used only with the guidance of a physician experienced in their use in children. Seizure disorders, which occur in a high percentage of autistic children, can be effectively treated with antiseizure medications.

While these therapies have led neither to a cure nor to eradication of autism, they have transformed the lives of autistic children and their parents dramatically. Twenty-five years ago, most such children faced a bleak future that led, more or less inevitably, to institutionalization. With the emergence of different treatment strategies, and with parental pressure on legislatures and social service agencies for more and better services, autistic individuals can now attend special schools, live at home, and look forward to better and more comprehensive attention to their special needs. Much more needs to be done, especially in research, where parental groups could be far more effective than they now are in *demanding* that federal funding agencies devote more of their resources to autism. Research funding for childhood disorders still receives much less of the resources than these disorders deserve. Only concerted, persistent action by parents, researchers, and other caregivers of autistic children can reverse this unacceptable state of affairs.

Reference

American Psychiatric Association. *Diagnostic and Statistical Manual of Mental Disorders.* (DSM-III-R.) Washington, D.C.: American Psychiatric Association, 1987.

Additional Sources

Campbell, M., Perry, R., Small, A. M., and Green, W. H. "Overview of Drug Treatment in Autism." In E. Schopler and G. Mesibov (eds.), *Neurobiological Issues in Autism.* New York: Plenum, 1987.

Chess, S. "Autism in Children with Congenital Rubella." *Journal of Autism and Childhood Schizophrenia,* 1971, *1* (1), 33-47.

Ciaranello, R. D., VandenBerg, S. R., and Anders, T. F. "Intrinsic and Extrinsic Determinants of Neuronal Development: Relations to Infantile Autism." *Journal of Autism and Developmental Disorders,* 1982, 12 (2), 115-146.

Ciaranello, R. D., and Wong, D. L. "Infantile Autism: Neurochemical and Neurobiological Considerations." In B. Hirsch, K. Grossfeld, and D. Lapidus (eds.), *Autism: A Transdisciplinary View of Current Research and Methods.* New York: Human Sciences Press, 1987.

Courchesne, E. "A Neurophysiological View of Autism." In E. Schopler and G. Mesibov (eds.), *Neurobiological Issues in Autism.* New York: Plenum, 1987.

Elliott, G. R., and Ciaranello, R. D. "Hypotheses of Childhood Psychoses." In E. Schopler and G. Mesibov (eds.), *Neurobiological Issues in Autism.* New York: Plenum, 1987.

Elliott, G. R., and Ciaranello, R. D. "Neurochemical Hypotheses of Childhood Psychoses." In E. Schopler and G. Mesibov (eds.), *Neurobiological Issues in Autism.* New York: Plenum, 1987.

Folstein, S., and Rutter, M. L. "Infantile Autism: A Genetic Study of 21 Twin Pairs." *Journal of Child Psychology and Psychiatry,* 1977, *18,* 297–321.

Folstein, S., and Rutter, M. L. "A Twin Study of Individuals with Infantile Autism." In M. L. Rutter and E. Schopler (eds.), *Autism: A Reappraisal of Concepts and Treatment.* New York: Plenum, 1978.

Folstein, S. E., and Rutter, M. L. "Autism: Familial Aggregation and Genetic Implications." In E. Schopler and G. Mesibov (eds.), *Neurobiological Issues in Autism.* New York: Plenum, 1987.

Folstein, S. E., and Rutter, M. L. "Autism: Familial Aggregation and Genetic Implications." *Journal of Autism and Developmental Disorders,* 1988, *18* (1), 3–30.

Hanson, D. R., and Gottesman, I. I. "The Genetics, If Any, of Infantile Autism and Childhood Schizophrenia." *Journal of Autism and Childhood Schizophrenia,* 1976, *6,* 209–234.

Ornitz, E. M., and Ritvo, E. R. "The Syndrome of Autism: A Critical Review." *American Journal of Psychiatry,* 1976, *133,* 609–621.

Rakic, P. "Specification of Cerebral Cortical Areas." *Science,* 1988, *241,* 170–176.

Rutter, M. L., and Bartak, L. "Causes of Infantile Autism: Some Considerations from Recent Research." *Journal of Autism and Childhood Schizophrenia,* 1971, *1* (1), 20–32.

Siegel, B., Anders, T., and Ciaranello, R. D. "Empirically Derived Subclassification of the Autistic Syndrome." *Journal of Autism and Developmental Disorders,* 1986, *16,* 275–293.

Smalley, S. L., Asarnow, R. F., and Spence, M. A. "Autism and Genetics." *Archives of General Psychiatry,* 1988, *45,* 953–961.

Spence, M. A., Ritvo, E. R., Marazita, M. L., Funderburk, S. L., Sparkes, R. S., and Freeman, B. J. "Gene Mapping Studies with the Syndrome of Autism." *Behavioral Genetics,* 1985, *15,* 1–13.

Todd, R. D., and Ciaranello, R. D. "Early Infantile Autism and the Childhood Psychoses." In P. J. Vinken, G. W. Bruyn, and H. L. Klawans (eds.), *Handbook of Clinical Neurology.* Amsterdam: Elsevier, 1985.

Wing, L. "Language, Social, and Cognitive Impairments in Autism and Severe Mental Retardation." *Journal of Autism and Developmental Disorders,* 1981, *11,* 31–44.

ROLAND D. CIARANELLO, the Nancy Friend Pritzker Professor of Psychiatry and Behavioral Sciences at Stanford University Medical School, is the recipient of a Research Career Scientist Award from the NIMH (MH 00219).

A behaviorally defined syndrome that is a neurobiological model for many other brain disorders, autism is a disorder characterized by specific behavioral and learning abnormalities associated with neural dysfunction and neuroanatomical abnormalities.

Autism

Eric Courchesne

Infantile autism is a behaviorally defined syndrome characterized by (1) a severe deficiency in both social knowledge and reciprocal social interaction (impaired social relatedness), (2) an abnormality in both verbal and non-verbal communication, (3) a markedly restricted repertoire of activities and interests, and (4) impaired cognition. (Also see the previous chapter.) First-time parents usually report their concern to a pediatrician when their child is around twenty-one months old, but more experienced parents often become aware of a problem when the child is only twelve months old or less. The pediatrician is crucial in the initial recognition and diagnosis of autism. Often a referral to a large medical center with a multidisciplinary team is necessary for an accurate diagnosis.

Children with autism are often assumed to be mentally retarded, yet at least 20 to 25 percent are not mentally retarded. About 25 percent of autistic children develop comorbid seizure activity, but no specific type of seizure has been identified as unique to autism. It is important for families and relatives to know that studies have shown that autistic children may have as much attachment to their caregivers as age- and IQ-matched mentally retarded children (Sigman and Mundy, 1989); however, autistic children show this attachment in unusual ways and at unexpected times.

Autism is a lifelong handicap. Yet with appropriate supportive services such as special educational programs, behavior modification, and psychosocial intervention, improvement in social, cognitive, and language skills is possible during the child's development. Pharmacological intervention has had little impact on the fundamental course of autism, even though modest progress has been made in improving the behavioral symptoms in some of these children.

NEW DIRECTIONS FOR MENTAL HEALTH SERVICES, no. 54, Summer 1992 ©Jossey-Bass Publishers

Etiology

It is likely that autism has several etiologies, but at present, the precise causal mechanisms are unknown (Nelson, 1991). Based on recent discoveries of neuroanatomical abnormalities in autism, the onset of the disorder may be as early as the second trimester of pregnancy (Courchesne, 1991; Bauman, 1991). (For a further discussion of the etiology of autism, see Chapter One.)

Two consistent kinds of scientific evidence have been accumulated to define autism as a true neurobiological disorder: recent neuroanatomical findings and event-related potential and neurobehavioral studies.

Neuroanatomy

Neuroanatomical findings related to the cerebellar region of the brain are perhaps the most important new data on autism. Autopsy data (Williams and others, 1980; Bauman and Kemper, 1985; Arin, Bauman, and Kemper, 1991) and brain imaging studies (Courchesne, Hesselink, Jernigan, and Yeung-Courchesne, 1987; Murakami and others, 1989; Courchesne, 1991) have now suggested that hypoplasia of the cerebellum occurs in some cases of autism. One of the most important aspects of these studies is that the precise location of these neuroanatomical abnormalities is consistent: both magnetic resonance imaging (MRI) and the autopsy studies identify the same region of the cerebellum as abnormal in autistic patients (Courchesne, 1991).[1] Another important aspect of the autopsy and brain imaging findings is the strong support that these studies give to the hypothesis that the demonstrable cerebellar abnormalities may occur as early as the second trimester in some cases, but the exact time of onset is still uncertain. The etiology of this structural damage is unknown.

An abnormality in the limbic system has also been reported in several autopsy cases of autism (Bauman, 1991). The abnormality was an increase in cell packing density: the neurons in the limbic system of the brain were too small and too close together. The functional significance of this finding is unknown. This abnormality was more severe in cases of mental retardation with autism than in a case of autism alone (M. L. Bauman, Autism Society of America lecture, July 10, 1991). Clearly, further research is needed to determine how common these limbic system abnormalities are in autism and whether they correlate more closely with autism per se or with mental retardation.

No damage of etiological significance has been found in any other subcortical or cortical structure in autopsy studies of autism (Bauman, 1991). In recent computerized tomographic (CT) and MRI studies on autistic patients, no pattern of abnormality in the cerebral cortex, thalamus, basal ganglia, and brain stem was found. If abnormalities do exist in these structures, they must apparently be of a subtle nature (Courchesne, 1991).

Pathophysiology

Event-related potential (ERP) reflects neural responses to a specific physical or psychological event. ERP is recorded by electrodes placed on a patient's scalp. In normal individuals, ERP responses to attention-related functions are well defined. But in autistic patients, ERP responses to attention-related functions are either diminished or totally absent. Such ERP studies, plus recent neurobehavioral studies, strongly suggest that autistic children have significant dysfunction in the neural mechanisms that underlie a human being's ability to capture, maintain, and shift attention (Courchesne, Akshoomoff, and Townsend, 1990). These ERP studies are extremely important because they suggest a relationship between social and behavioral dysfunction in autistic children on the one hand and reproducible, measurable electrical and anatomical abnormalities in the brain on the other. Recent neurobehavioral studies, designed to determine the specific relationship between a particular site or system in the brain and a person's behavior, point to cerebellar damage as the reason for deficits in shifting attention (Akshoomoff and Courchesne, 1992; Courchesne and others, 1992).

In addition, newer brain imaging studies—positron emission tomography (PET) scans—support the ERP studies that demonstrate diminished attention-related functioning in autistic patients. The PET scans confirm reduced activity or function in the frontal-parietal regions and in the neostriatum and thalamic regions of the brain in autistic children as compared to normal controls (Horowitz, Rumsey, Grady, and Rapoport, 1988).

The link between abnormal neurochemistry and autism is inconclusive. Hyperserotonemia (elevated serotonin blood levels) is observed in 33 percent of autistic children. Also, elevated levels of homovanillic acid, a metabolite of dopamine, have been documented in the cerebrospinal fluid of some autistic patients. But attempts to understand the significance of these findings have been unsuccessful so far.

Research Directions

Considering all the scientific data available, autism is a neurobiological model for many other brain disorders: specific behavioral and learning abnormalities are directly associated with neural dysfunction and neuroanatomical abnormalities. More research on the neurobiological abnormalities related to autism in the following four areas is essential: (1) Most important would be molecular genetic studies to explain the anatomical abnormalities. (2) ERP and neurobehavioral studies in combination with brain imaging are essential to explain the functional significance of the anatomical abnormalities described so far. (3) Autopsy and brain imaging studies are needed to verify the anatomical deficits already described and to determine whether other brain sites might also be damaged. A full explanation of the characteristics of autism will require taking into account more than cerebellar damage, because it is likely that impairment in other brain sites combines with the cerebellar damage to create the full array of characteristics of autism. (4) Research is needed to better understand the biochemical abnormalities (for example, hyperserotonemia) that may be associated with a subgroup of autistic children.

Research in these four areas could not only lead to better educational, behavioral, and pharmacological treatment but may also lead to an explanation of the etiology of autism. When the etiology is understood, scientific research could potentially proceed to prevention of this neurological disorder.

Note

1. Although structural cerebellar abnormalities are present in many individuals with autism, not all investigators have reported similar results. This, therefore, remains an area of active study.

References

Akshoomoff, N. A., and Courchesne, E. "A Role of the Cerebellum in Cognitive Operations." Unpublished manuscript, University of California, San Diego, 1992.

Arin, D. M., Bauman, M. L., and Kemper, T. L. "The Distribution of Purkinje Cell Loss in the Cerebellum in Autism." *Neurology,* 1991, *41,* 307.

Bauman, M. L. "Microscopic Neuroanatomic Abnormalities in Autism." *Pediatrics,* 1991, *87,* 791–796.

Bauman, M. L., and Kemper, T. L. "Histoanatomic Observations of the Brain in Early Infantile Autism." *Neurology,* 1985, *35,* 866–874.

Courchesne, E. "Neuroanatomic Imaging in Autism." *Pediatrics,* 1991, *87,* 781–790.

Courchesne, E., Akshoomoff, N. A., and Townsend, J. "Recent Advances in Autism." *Pediatrics,* 1990, *2,* 685–693.

Courchesne, E., Akshoomoff, N. A., Townsend, J. P., Yeung-Courchesne, R., Lincoln, A. J., James, H. E., Haas, R. H., Schreibman, L., and Lau, L. "Impairment in Shifting Attention in Autistic and Cerebellar Patients." Unpublished manuscript, University of California, San Diego, 1992.

Courchesne, E., Hesselink, J. R., Jernigan, T. J., and Yeung-Courchesne, R. "Abnormal Neuroanatomy in a Nonretarded Person with Autism: Unusual Findings with Magnetic Resonance Imaging." *Archives of Neurology,* 1987, *44,* 335–341.

Horowitz, B., Rumsey, J., Grady, C., and Rapoport, S. "The Cerebral Metabolic Landscape in Autism." *Archives of Neurology,* 1988, *45,* 749–755.

Murakami, J. W., Courchesne, E., Press, G. A., Yeung-Courchesne, R., and Hesselink, J. R. "Reduced Cerebellar Hemisphere Size and Its Relationship to Vermal Hypoplasia in Autism." *Archives of Neurology,* 1989, *46,* 689–694.

Nelson, K. B. "An Update on Autism: A Developmental Disorder." *Pediatrics* (suppl.), 1991, *87,* i–vi, 751–795.

Sigman, M., and Mundy, P. "Social Attachments in Autistic Children." *Journal of the American Academy of Child and Adolescent Psychiatry,* 1989, *28,* 74–81.

Williams, R. S., Hauser, S. L., Purpura, D. P., De Long, R., and Swisher, C. N. "Autism and Mental Retardation: Neuropathologic Studies Performed in Four Retarded Persons with Autistic Behavior." *Archives of Neurology,* 1980, *37,* 749–753.

ERIC COURCHESNE is professor of neurosciences in the School of Medicine at the University of California, San Diego, where he specializes in developmental neurosciences.

Obsessive-compulsive disorder, a neurobiological disease associated with abnormalities in the basal ganglia, responds with some success to behavior modification and also to new pharmacological therapies.

Obsessive-Compulsive Disorder

Judith L. Rapoport

Obsessive-compulsive disorder (OCD) is a severe, chronic, biologically rooted syndrome. In the last decade, a new biological model of OCD has rapidly emerged. OCD manifests itself through obsessions (recurrent, persistent ideas, thoughts, or impulses that are intrusive and senseless) or compulsions (repetitive behaviors performed in response to an obsession, or according to certain rules, or in a stereotyped fashion, and perceived by the person as irrational). Exhibit 3.1 lists the most common symptoms of obsessions and compulsions in children and adolescents.

Three major features distinguish OCD patients from people who may have just some aspects of OCD: (1) OCD patients' behaviors and thought patterns become so time consuming and demanding that they interfere with their lives to a considerable degree. (2) The obsessive-compulsive component in OCD patients is limited; in most *other* aspects of life the patients' behaviors are quite normal and reasonable. (3) OCD patients realize that their OCD behavior is senseless but they cannot control it; therefore, they suffer painfully from their consciousness of the ridiculous nature of their OCD behaviors, which are programmed against their will.

At one time, it was thought that OCD was a relatively rare disorder. This misconception was largely due to the fact that so many persons with OCD avoided medical or psychiatric help. It is typical for OCD patients to conceal their symptoms and suffering for years before seeking medical intervention. In part because persons with OCD understand that their rituals and thoughts are senseless, they go to great lengths to conceal them. Only when the OCD symptoms become so severe that they interfere with school, work, or social obligations is an individual with OCD likely to seek medical help. Another important factor contributing to the underestimate

New Directions for Mental Health Services, no. 54, Summer 1992 © Jossey-Bass Publishers

Exhibit 3.1. Most Common Symptoms of OCD in Children and Adolescents

Obsessions
1. Concern with dirt, germs, or environmental toxins
2. Something terrible happening (fire, death, illness)
3. Symmetry, order, or exactness
4. Concern or disgust with bodily wastes or secretions
5. Religious obsessions
6. Lucky or unlucky numbers
7. Forbidden, aggressive, or perverse sexual thoughts, images, or impulses
8. Fear of harming self or others
9. Intrusive nonsense sounds, words, or music.

Compulsions
1. Excessive or ritualized hand washing, showering, bathing, or grooming
2. Repeating rituals such as going in or out of doors or rising and sitting in a chair
3. Checking doors, locks, stove, appliances, car brake, and so on
4. Touching
5. Counting
6. Hoarding or collecting
7. Ritualistic cleaning of household items or inanimate objects
8. Ritualistic measures to prevent harm to self or others
9. Rituals to remove contact with dirt or contaminants
10. Miscellaneous rituals (writing, speaking, reading).

---

of the prevalence of OCD and to OCD patients' avoidance of psychiatric attention is the fact that traditional psychotherapy and family therapy are ineffective in treating this disease.

Most recent studies now suggest that OCD is not rare and may affect 2 percent of the entire U.S. population. From one-third to one-half of all OCD victims begin to experience their symptoms in childhood or adolescence. Many well-documented cases of OCD began as early as age three years. One of the most important observations about OCD is the striking uniformity of symptoms in children and adults. This strongly suggests a biological etiology for this disease.

Etiology, Neuroanatomy, and Pathophysiology

The exact etiology and pathophysiology of OCD are unknown. Yet a substantial body of scientific data implicates a dysfunction in the basal ganglia of the brain. It is also probable that the serotonergic neurotransmitter system is involved in OCD.

Three general features of OCD strongly support the conclusion that OCD is a neurobiological disorder: (1) There is the remarkable finding that OCD symptoms are similar in both the child-adolescent and adult populations. (2) The disease is more prevalent among relatives of OCD patients than in the general population. (3) There is a strong association between

OCD and certain other neurobiological disorders. For example, about 20 percent of OCD patients also display motor tic disorders (see Chapter Four) that have a strong neurobiological etiology.

All the scientific studies on OCD, which incorporate a wide diversity of approaches, have implicated the basal ganglia as an important brain site associated with OCD. The main findings can be summarized as follows: (1) OCD occurs in conjunction with several other neurological disorders that involve the basal ganglia, including Sydenham's chorea, postencephalitic Parkinson's disease, and toxic lesions of the basal ganglia. (2) Standard neurological testing designed to identify specific anatomical brain regions indicates that OCD patients consistently have functional deficits in the frontal lobes or the basal ganglia, or in both of these brain regions. (3) One computerized axial tomography (CAT) study of the brain of OCD patients has shown a decrease in the volume of the caudate nucleus (a region of the basal ganglia) compared to a control group of patients who did not have OCD. (4) Positron emission tomography (PET) scan studies have shown brain images in which the activity of glucose metabolism is higher in the frontal lobes and in the cingulate pathway (which connects the frontal lobes to the basal ganglia) or in the basal ganglia in OCD patients compared to normal controls. (5) Pharamacological agents that block the serotonergic system are the *most* effective therapy for OCD. Serotonergic neurons are widely distributed throughout the brain, but they are concentrated in the basal ganglia. Therefore, an impressive body of scientific evidence supports the conclusion that OCD is a distinct biological disorder associated with abnormalities in the basal ganglia region of the brain.

The evidence that OCD is associated with the serotonergic neurotransmitter system is indirect but persuasive. Three pharmacological therapies have documented usefulness in the treatment of OCD: clomipramine (Anafranil), fluvoxamine, and fluoxetine (Prozac). All three block the reuptake of serotonin in the complex interaction that occurs at the neurotransmitter synapse level. Clomipramine also affects the action of other neurotransmitters, such as the dopaminergic system. Thus, it is possible that other neurotransmitters are involved in OCD. In sum, although the exact pathophysiology of OCD is unknown, the most recent scientific evidence supports a biological model in which OCD is a disease triggered by abnormal functioning of the basal ganglia–frontal lobe interaction. These abnormal interactions are conveyed by pathways mediated by the serotonin neurotransmitter system and perhaps also by the dopaminergic system.

Medical Management of OCD

Many older forms of therapy for OCD have been a failure. In particular, psychotherapy, family counseling, and most older drugs used for treating anxiety and depression have been unsuccessful. At least 50 percent or more of OCD patients treated with psychotherapy or older drug therapies still suffer from the disease seven to twenty years after the completion of such therapies.

On the other hand, two very different kinds of treatment have been effective in dealing with OCD. The first is behavior therapy. Although such therapy has been criticized, it has proven to be effective in some severe cases of OCD. It must be emphasized that behavior therapy seems to be more effective in treating compulsions than obsessions. The second kind of efficacious therapy for OCD is pharmacological. Three pharmacological therapies have been successful in the treatment of OCD: clomipramine, fluvoxamine, and fluoxetine. All three inhibit the re-uptake of serotonin in the neuronal synapse.

The scientific study and treatment of OCD should serve as a model for other neurobiological illnesses. At least fourteen *prospective* scientific double-blind studies have demonstrated the clinical efficacy of clomipramine in treating OCD. This kind of scientific clinical research scrutiny should be applied to *all* other forms of therapy for severe childhood and adolescent psychiatric illnesses.

Research Directions

More research using the techniques of CAT and PET scanning of OCD patients is clearly indicated to more clearly define the role of the frontal lobes and the basal ganglia and the interaction between these two anatomical sites in this disease. Also, further research should be devoted to the interactions between the serotonergic and dopaminergic neurotransmitter systems and OCD, which may lead to improved pharmacological therapy for this neurobiological disorder.

Additional Sources

Jenike, M. A., Baer, L., and Minichiello, W. E. (eds.). *Obsessive-Compulsive Disorders: Theory and Management.* (2nd ed.) Chicago: Year Book Medical Publishers, 1990.

Rapoport, J. L. *The Boy Who Couldn't Stop Washing: The Experience and Treatment of Obsessive-Compulsive Disorder.* New York: Dutton, 1989.

Rapoport, J. L. (ed.). *Obsessive-Compulsive Disorder in Children and Adolescents.* Washington, D.C.: American Psychiatric Press, 1989.

JUDITH L. RAPOPORT is chief of the Child Psychiatry Branch at the National Institute of Mental Health.

Tourette's syndrome, a familial neurological disease of childhood onset, can respond to some pharmacological treatments.

Tourette's Syndrome

James F. Leckman

Named for Gilles de la Tourette (1857–1904), the French physician who first described this symptom cluster in 1885, Tourette's syndrome (TS) is an uncommon familial neurological disease. Usually a lifelong disorder of childhood onset, TS is characterized by waxing and waning motor and phonic tics plus complex behavioral symptoms. TS affects more boys than girls by a factor of at least three to one. Prevalence estimates indicate that between one and six per 1,000 boys may have TS. In its most severe form, TS can be disabling. Yet many people with TS live full lives despite their symptoms. Pharmacological therapy helps many patients, but unwanted side effects can limit the long-term value of medication.

TS often begins when a five- to seven-year-old begins to experience transient bouts of tics of the face or head like eye blinking, grimacing, or shoulder jerks. In some cases, the tics cease after a few weeks and the child may be symptom free for weeks or months. Later, when symptoms recur, they may be more frequent and forceful and involve other areas of the body.

Simple motor tics are sudden, lightning-like movements, usually purposeless in character. In time, the tics, which can involve almost any part of the body's voluntary motor functioning, may seem to be done "on purpose." In fact, the TS child has little or no control over them. Some children can "suppress" some of their tics for a few minutes. Others have no control at all. Simple phonic tics like sniffing, throat clearing, hissing, or barking usually begin to appear after the motor tics, when the child is around age nine to twelve. Later, more complex tics—like the ejaculation of syllables, words, or phrases—can emerge. Coprolalia, which involves uttering obscene words or phrases out of context, occurs in 20 to 30 percent of patients referred for treatment.

NEW DIRECTIONS FOR MENTAL HEALTH SERVICES, no. 54, Summer 1992 © Jossey-Bass Publishers

Once established, the tics tend to wax and wane in severity. Like other chronic diseases, TS is stress-responsive, so that some exacerbations of TS tics can be directly traced to increased stresses. At other times, TS symptoms seem to wax and wane due to underlying biological factors that are not yet well understood.

In late adolescence or early adulthood, tics often abate. Although an adult with TS may have motor and phonic tics, the tics tend to be less frequent and forceful. Paradoxically, the most severe cases of TS occur in adults.

TS Plus Obsessive-Compulsive Disorder and Attention Deficit Hyperactivity Disorder

Evidence from family and twin studies suggests an intrinsic relationship between TS and some forms of obsessive-compulsive disorder (OCD). In families with TS, there is a much higher incidence of OCD than would be expected. This leads to the hypothesis that a person with a genetic predisposition to TS may also be predisposed to certain kinds of TS-related OCD. For example, females in TS families tend to have OCD alone rather than TS plus OCD. Therefore, OCD clinics and psychiatrists treating people with OCD should get a detailed personal history plus a family history of tic disorder, because the OCD patient may have a TS-related OCD instead of the separate diagnosis of OCD alone. Identifying and separating TS-related OCD from non-TS OCD may lead to a better understanding of the pathophysiology of OCD in general. Also, some patients with OCD plus some tic symptoms who do not respond to the usual OCD drugs may experience improvement of their OCD when treated with small doses of TS neuroleptics like pimozide.

At least 50 percent of TS patients who seek medical help also have attention deficit hyperactivity disorder (ADHD). It is unknown if ADHD is an alternate expression (like OCD) of a biological vulnerability to TS or if ADHD is simply a comorbid condition that shares common aspects with the pathophysiology of TS.

Etiology, Neuroanatomy, and Pathophysiology

The etiology and pathophysiology of TS are unknown. Genetic and twin studies suggest that in some families, hereditary factors are involved in the vertical transmission of TS: the pattern is that of an autosomal dominant gene transmitted from one generation to the next. But even in people with a genetic predisposition to TS, nongenetic factors (stress, anxiety, and possibly stimulant medication) may be crucial for the expression of the disease. Perinatal factors (like lower birth weight and complications during pregnancy) may also play an important role in determining the severity of the disease.

Drug studies, brain autopsy studies, and brain imaging scans have implicated abnormal functioning in specific brain regions associated with TS. These include certain neural pathways that link cortical regions (prefrontal, cingulate, motor, sensorimotor) with the basal ganglia (caudate nucleus, putamen, globus pallidus), thalamic nuclei, and certain more posterior caudal structures (substantia nigra, ventral tegmental area, periaquiductal gray matter). These studies represent only the beginning of an integrated model of structure and function that may ultimately account for the puzzling symptoms that TS patients must live with every day of their lives.

It is likely that TS symptoms are mediated by neurotransmitters and neuromodulators in the brain, but no single neurochemical model has yet emerged as a dominant working hypothesis to explain these symptoms. Still, some neurochemical systems have been repeatedly implicated in the pathophysiology of TS. Central dopaminergic systems have been tied to TS via the following data: (1) the proven efficacy of dopaminergic blocking agents (haloperidol, fluphenazine, pimozide), (2) the suppression of tics by inhibitors of dopamine synthesis, and (3) exacerbation of tics with agents that may increase dopaminergic activity like methylphenidate, amphetamine, and cocaine. The relationships of the serotonergic, noradrenergic, endogeneous opioid, cholinergic, and GABAergic (gamma-aminobutyric acid) systems to TS remain suggestive. Whatever the pathophysiology of TS, it probably includes the direct involvement of the dopaminergic systems set in the context of one or more neurophysiological pathways implicated by the autopsy and brain imaging studies discussed above.

Medical Management of TS as a Chronic Disease; Prognosis

TS is a chronic, incurable disease. But education, support services, and medical treatment can play crucial roles in improving a TS patient's quality of life. Because of the variability in the expression of TS vulnerability, many TS patients can lead productive lives with or without medical intervention. Families first seek medical help when a child's tics increase in frequency and severity. We initially give the family as much education as they want or are ready to receive. We encourage families to contact the Tourette Syndrome Association (TSA), a support group of families and people with TS, which can give families much more understanding, support, and information about living with this chronic illness than professionals can. While a doctor can give the diagnosis of and education about TS, pharmacological treatment, advice, and support, families of TS patients must deal with school systems, health and medical insurance systems, government agencies, and relatives and friends, all of which have little or no knowledge about TS. Support groups can be crucial in helping families and patients cope with these aspects of life.

Although most children with TS are first brought to a doctor because of the frequency and severity of their symptoms, we usually do not prescribe medications until we establish a clear picture of the symptoms. TS symptoms tend to wax and wane; many patients' symptoms improve in a few weeks without pharmacological intervention. In our experience, about 30 to 40 percent of all TS cases never need medication. In childhood TS or TS-related OCD, we usually keep in close telephone contact with families and schedule follow-up appointments at three- to six-month intervals. We counsel TS patients to avoid certain medications or drugs like methylphenidate (Ritalin), amphetamines, cocaine, and androgenic steroids that can exacerbate tic behavior. We also advise parents to minimize the TS child's exposure to decongestants and over-the-counter cold preparations because of their potential to make tics worse.

For patients who need medications, neuroleptics that selectively block dopamine receptors in various brain regions can effectively relieve some TS symptoms. In eight- to twelve-week trials of haloperidol (Haldol) or pimozide (Orap), a 60 to 80 percent reduction in both motor and phonic tics has been consistently documented. Due to the potential side effects of neuroleptics, including weight gain, cognitive blunting, and tardive dyskinesia (a different kind of involuntary movement disorder), we use the smallest dose possible that can improve symptoms. Some TS patients show no significant response to the neuroleptics. Others respond at first but seem to develop a tolerance later on so that symptoms recur, despite continued treatment. Increasing the dose does not always recapture the drug's useful effects—and may increase its unwanted side effects.

Newer, more effective drugs for TS are needed. A promising one is clonidine: it can be effective and has fewer long-term side effects than the neuroleptics. But response to it is less predictable; only about a third of patients improve significantly in the first twelve weeks of treatment.

During all medication trials, we encourage families to keep in close contact with the physician, either by telephone or through clinic visits. It is important to be patient during such a trial. But if both the doctor and the family judge that a medication is ineffective, and if it has been given a reasonable trial, the medication should be discontinued.

Because TS is a chronic disease, it can have damaging psychological and, more rarely, physical effects on children, even if they are bright and have other talents. Components of a multidisciplinary support system for a TS child include (1) a physician familiar with the child's medical history who will provide consistent, continuous long-term care and support; (2) a working partnership between the doctor and the caring family; and (3) a supportive educational system (special education programs, if necessary) that can work with the family and physician.

The key factor in TS prognosis is usually not the severity of the symptoms but how well the child can maintain the course of normal development. If TS symptoms occur while a child maintains the developmental demands of his or her age (family, peer relations, school, and so on), the prognosis is usually much better. Every effort in terms of special education and support services should be made to help the child achieve maximum development, despite the severity of the TS.

Research Directions

More research on the genetics and neurobiology of TS will be crucial. If the details of the underlying genetic vulnerability and neurobiological substrates for TS were better understood, more effective drugs could be developed with fewer side effects. Better anatomical studies using state-of-the-art brain imaging techniques that identify specific brain regions correlated with TS should be funded. Ultimately, it will also be important to define the nongenetic factors that contribute to the expression of the disease.

Until we can identify the precise genetic abnormality responsible for TS and develop techniques to correct it, we encourage research on a full range of interventions. As science develops new neuropharmacological drugs, it will be important for the United States to support well-designed clinical trials to scientifically investigate their efficacy in TS. We also need to focus on environmental factors (including prenatal care) that may reduce the severity of this genetic, neurobiological disease.

Additional Sources

Cohen, D., Brunn, R. D., and Leckman, J. F. (eds.). *Tourette's Syndrome and Tic Disorders: Clinical Understanding and Treatment.* New York: Wiley, 1988.

Comings, D. E. *Tourette's Syndrome and Human Behavior.* Duarte, Calif.: Hope Press, 1990.

Lees, A. J. *Tics and Related Disorders.* Edinburgh, Scotland: Churchill Livingstone, 1985.

Shapiro, A. K., Shapiro, E. S., Young, J. G., and Feinberg, T. E. *Gilles de la Tourette Syndrome.* New York: Raven Press, 1988.

JAMES F. LECKMAN is Neison Harris Professor of Child Psychiatry and Pediatrics at Yale University School of Medicine.

The etiology of bipolar disorder (BD) has a complex genetic component; juvenile- and adolescent-onset BD may be expressing the most genotypically severe form of the illness.

Bipolar Disorder

Michael Strober

The susceptibility of certain individuals to pathological swings in mood between elation and depression has been recognized as a human affliction for many centuries. According to modern epidemiological studies, manic-depression or bipolar disorder (BD) is estimated to affect nearly 1 out of every 100 in the population. Today, after decades of relative neglect, BD is once again the subject of intense interest, scientific scrutiny, and efforts to develop more effective maintenance therapies.

Clinical Description and Course of Illness

The extremes of mood, activity, and cognition that characterize manic and depressive states vary in severity and duration. In mania, the mood can be one of gaiety or irritability, coupled with extraordinary mental and physical energy and boundless self-confidence. But because manic behavior is unfocused, impulse-driven, and senseless, it ultimately produces great hardship and disruption. In contrast to the manic high, depressive states in BD are characterized by profound despondency, a sharp reduction in mental and physical activity, alterations in sleep and appetite, and confused ruminative thinking. In some people, episodes run their course in a matter of weeks, yet episodes lasting several months are not uncommon.

The first signs of BD usually appear in the early to mid twenties, but there is considerable variability in age of onset. Twenty-five percent or more of affected individuals suffer their first attack as adolescents.

Once the illness surfaces, the subsequent course in any one patient is difficult, if not impossible, to predict. For some, BD is a chronic handicapping illness with frequently recurring manic and depressive episodes

NEW DIRECTIONS FOR MENTAL HEALTH SERVICES, no. 54, Summer 1992 © Jossey-Bass Publishers

throughout life. For others, the interval between episodes may be years, although long-term follow-up studies indicate that the majority of people with BD will experience at least several episodes. Follow-up studies also suggest that as the illness progresses, the time between episode recurrences tends to shorten. Sometimes episodes are precipitated by stressful life events; this may be more likely early in the course of BD. As the illness progresses, the role of life events in triggering attacks seems to decrease as episodes wax and wane in a more autonomous, spontaneous manner.

Development in Children and Adolescents

Whether or not BD assumes a somewhat different appearance when it develops early in life is a matter of some controversy. Evidence from several studies suggests that episode severity may be greater in juvenile patients than in adults, reflected in more prominent psychomotor slowing (in the depressive pole) and more frequent hallucinations and delusions. However, not all studies agree on this point.

By most accounts, the core manic-depressive syndrome is rare before puberty. Nonetheless, some have asserted that BD can unfold in very young children in the form of severe emotional lability coupled with hyperactivity and unusually erratic patterns of boisterousness and depressive behavior. It would be fair to state that present knowledge of the early precursors of BD is too limited to permit reliable discrimination of pre-bipolar states from other common nonaffective disturbances of childhood.

Etiology and Pathogenesis

It is now well established that BD runs in families, strongly suggesting a genetic component to the etiology of BD. Modern genetic studies show that relatives of BD patients are at least three times more likely to develop some form of major affective illness, compared to the general population. Evidence from twin and adoption studies supports the involvement of genetic influences, yet all indications are that the inheritance of BD is complex and will be far more difficult to pin down than was previously believed. Some authorities no longer hypothesize that BD is a single genetic entity but, rather, a final common pathway for several different autosomal or X-linked abnormal genes. Of interest here is increasing evidence that bipolars with juvenile onset of their illness have an unusually heavy loading of illness among their relatives, suggesting that onset in childhood or adolescence may be expressing the most genotypically severe form of BD.

No single biological abnormality has been established thus far as having causal significance in BD, and specific regional disturbances in brain functioning have yet to be implicated as points of vulnerability. However, numerous pathophysiological and pathogenic mechanisms have been advanced during the past two decades. The most widely investigated of these hypotheses concerns the involvement of abnormal oscillations in neurotransmitter systems regulating mood and biological rhythms. Although a variety of methodological problems preclude any straightforward inter- pretation of these data, there are indications of altered noradrenergic and cellular membrane processes in bipolar patients. The question of neuroan- atomical localization of a BD-causing lesion or deficit is an intriguing one. While data are sparse, brain imaging and neuropathological studies are suggestive of left frontotemporal hemispheric dysfunction in depression, and of right hemisphere abnormalities in manic states. These anatomical data are not free of methodological problems, and it is doubtless premature to assume that specific structural or laterality deficits have single, direct etiological effects on BD.

Clinical Management

While there is no known cure for BD, a variety of medications have demon- strated value in the acute and long-term management of the condition. Lithium remains the most widely prescribed treatment for acute manic epi- sodes; it is sometimes administered in conjunction with neuroleptic drugs when control of agitation, impulsivity, or psychosis is necessary. This com- bination is effective in about 80 percent of adults with BD, with improvement seen in two to six weeks on average. For patients who respond poorly or min- imally to this regimen, other medications are available that may be beneficial. These include anticonvulsants such as carbamazepine (Tegretol), clonaze- pam (Klonopin), and valproic acid (Depakene); thyroid hormones, which may be particularly effective for rapidly cycling bipolar patients; and calcium channel blockers such as verapamil (Calan, Isoptin).

A wide variety of agents are available for the treatment of acute bipolar depressions, including tricyclics and monoamine oxidase inhibitors and newer drugs such as buproprion (Wellbutrin) and fluoxetine (Prozac). Opin- ion is divided on which class of antidepressant drug is best suited for the treatment of bipolar depression and whether or not antidepressants increase the risk of precipitating manic attacks.

Because of the cyclical nature of BD, the most crucial treatment issue concerns long-term preventive maintenance therapy. In studies of adults with BD, lithium and carbamazepine have been shown to be effective in reducing the risk of relapse over time. But approximately 35 percent of patients still have recurrences of severe symptoms, even when they are maintained on adequate levels of medication.

What remains unknown at present is how well these drugs work in treating acute attacks of manic-depression in the juvenile patient and whether they offer benefits in longer-term management. Few data are avail- able to address these clinically important questions in children and adolescents. However, the few studies published to date suggest that children and adolescents may respond less dramatically to antidepressant compounds than adults do. On the other hand, one recently completed study suggests that adolescents with BD who discontinue lithium maintenance therapy are at substantially greater risk for relapsing than those who remain compliant with maintenance treatment.

Future Prospects

Efforts to map a gene, or genes, conferring vulnerability to BD are proceeding at a rapid pace. If this quest proves successful, it will be possible to better understand the underlying pathophysiology of BD and to devise treatment interventions targeted to specific aspects of vulnerability. A further crucial need is to elucidate biological and psychosocial determinants and correlates of juvenile onset of illness and to clarify the impact of early onset on later educational, occupational, and psychological functioning. Increasingly sophisticated investigation of biological processes via neuroimaging and neurochemical techniques holds great promise for advancing our knowledge of central nervous system functioning, as well as of abnormalities at the chemical and intracellular levels, that may create susceptibility to BD.

Additional Sources

Goodwin, F. K., and Jamison, K. R. *Manic-Depressive Illness.* New York: Oxford University Press, 1990.

Last, C., and Hersen, M. *Handbook of Child Psychiatric Diagnosis.* New York: Wiley, 1989.

Strober, M., Morrell, W., Lampert, C., and Burroughs, J. "Relapse Following Discontinuation of Lithium Maintenance Therapy in Adolescents with Bipolar I Illness: A Naturalistic Study." *American Journal of Psychiatry,* 1990, *147,* 457–461.

Winokur, G., Clayton, P. J., and Reich, T. *Manic-Depressive Illness.* St. Louis, Mo.: Mosby, 1969.

MICHAEL STROBER is professor of psychiatry, School of Medicine, University of California at Los Angeles, and director, Child and Adolescent Mood Disorders Program, UCLA Neuropsychiatric Institute and Hospital.

Major depressive disorder (MDD) is now an accepted disorder in children and adolescents; genetic studies and data that support a dysregulation of one or more neurotransmitter systems suggest that biological factors play an important role in MDD in children and adolescents.

Major Depressive Disorder

David A. Brent

Fifteen years ago, major depressive disorder (MDD) was not universally recognized as a specific disease in children or adolescents. Now, however, MDD is an established, accepted disorder in both children and adolescents. Indeed, there are very few phenomenological differences in the syndrome picture of MDD in children and adolescents versus MDD in adults. The clinical differences between MDD in children and adolescents versus MDD in adults are due to developmental changes rather than to the nature of the symptoms.

MDD is relatively rare; the estimates of the frequency of this disorder range from 1.8 to 2.5 percent in prepubertal children and from 4.4 to 6.4 percent in adolescents. MDD is equally common among prepubertal males and females but is more common in adolescent females than in adolescent males. According to the DSM-III-R (American Psychiatric Association, 1987), the diagnosis of MDD requires at least two weeks of nearly constant depressed mood plus any four additional symptoms listed in Exhibit 6.1 (or any three additional symptoms for children under age six).

Exhibit 6.1. Additional Symptoms of MDD

Coincident with depressed mood, at least four of the following symptoms (or three symptoms for children under six years) must be present for a clinical diagnosis of MDD:

1. Change in appetite or weight (either increased or decreased); in children, a failure to make age-appropriate weight gain
2. Insomnia or hypersomnia nearly every day
3. Observable psychomotor agitation or retardation
4. Loss of interest or pleasure; diminished libido
5. Loss of energy; fatigue nearly every day
6. Feelings of worthlessness or inappropriate guilt
7. Difficulty concentrating, indecision
8. Recurrent thoughts of death or suicidal ideation or behavior.

A history of manic symptomatology in a person with MDD confers the diagnosis of bipolar affective disorder (see Chapter Five). The rest of this chapter is confined to MDD exclusive of bipolar disorder.

MDD must be distinguished from dysthymia, a milder, more chronic form of affective illness, and from adjustment disorder with depressed mood, which has a less severe mood disturbance and fewer symptoms and is self-limited. Numerous other disorders may also be associated with mood disturbance, including learning disabilities, attention deficit disorder, separation anxiety, anorexia nervosa, and drug and alcohol abuse.

MDD in children and adolescents generally runs a chronic and recurrent course. If untreated, an episode of MDD lasts an average of seven months. Approximately 40 percent of depressed children experience a relapse within two years. The earlier the age of onset of the first episode of MDD, the greater the risk of recurrences. As many as one-third of prepubertal children with MDD may show psychotic features such as hallucinations, delusions, and paranoid ideation. Even after recovery, most prepubertal children show significant social impairment. In adolescents, the sequelae of MDD may include tobacco, alcohol, and drug abuse; the development of antisocial behavior; and interference with interpersonal relationships. In both male and female adolescents, MDD confers a significantly increased risk for suicide.

Parents frequently mislabel true MDD as the "ups and downs" of childhood or adolescence. Parents should consider MDD for any child with unexplained somatic complaints, a drop in school performance, social withdrawal, apathy and loss of interest, increased irritability or tearfulness, sleep or appetite changes, and suicidal behavior or ideation. Pediatricians and parents should be particularly aware of a family history of MDD or bipolar disorder because this will increase the risk of MDD in the child.

Etiology and Pathophysiology

While the etiology of MDD in children and adolescents is unknown, it is likely that biological factors play an important role, based on both family-genetic studies and data that support a dysregulation of one or several neurotransmitter systems.

For MDD in children and adolescents, family-genetic factors are of paramount importance. Childhood-, adolescent-, and young adult–onset MDD tend to cluster in the same family. For patients experiencing onset of MDD before age twenty, about 24 percent of first-degree relatives will also have a major affective disorder. Despite the clear familial nature of childhood- and adolescent-onset MDD, it is likely that the genetic transmission of this disorder is complex and multifactorial.

In adults, the role of various neurotransmitter systems—noradrenergic, dopaminergic, serotonergic—in depression is strongly supported by a variety of studies. For example, numerous chemical challenge studies in adults suggest that the alpha$_2$-adrenergic receptor responsiveness is diminished in at least a subgroup of depressed patients. (Challenge studies involve administering a certain drug or chemical under very controlled conditions and then observing the response to the drug—such as the amount of growth hormone production when certain chemicals are given.) The level of melatonin, which is produced by noradrenergic neurons in the superior cervical ganglia, is reduced in depressed adult patients. Most of these adult studies suggest a defect in the regulation of the noradrenergic system. In addition, several dopamine receptor agonist studies and some dopamine metabolite studies suggest that the dopamine neurotransmitter system may play a role in some adult patients with depression. The mechanism of action for many of the known efficacious antidepressant therapies—including imipramine, fluoxetine, and electroshock therapy—strongly implicates the serotonergic neurotransmitter system in adult depression. The precise mechanism of interaction of any of these neurotransmitter systems with adult depression is unknown, but the weight of evidence clearly points to numerous neurochemical abnormalities that underlie adult-onset depression.

Although there is a substantial body of data supporting abnormal neurotransmitter function in adult depression, this has not been as extensively investigated in children and adolescents with depression. This is largely for two reasons: (1) MDD has only recently been defined for the younger age groups and (2) there are still very few researchers studying this disorder in children and adolescents. Despite the relative paucity of clinical and research studies on MDD in children and adolescents, the available data also implicate multiple neurotransmitter abnormalities in childhood- and adolescent-onset MDD. For example, during a major depression, prepubertal children hyposecrete growth hormone during an insulin-induced hypoglycemia challenge, compared to nondepressed psychiatrically ill patients and to normal controls. These altered growth hormone responses are also found in nondepressed children who are the offspring of depressed parents, suggesting that these changes may be part of a set of intrinsic biological traits predisposing to depression. Other challenge studies with clonidine and L-dopa show a lowered growth hormone response in depressed prepubertal boys, compared to normal controls. Also, MDD-onset adolescents with suicidal ideation or behavior exhibit a decreased growth hormone response to desipramine challenge and alteration of secretion of growth hormone (decreased) and cortisol (increased) shortly after sleep onset. Nocturnal growth hormone secretion in adolescents with MDD is significantly disturbed, compared to normal controls. As in the adult population, these studies suggest a possible dysregulation of the serotonergic, noradrenergic, and dopaminergic neurotransmitter systems in the childhood and adolescent population with MDD. Most important, the findings of all of these studies *document a biologically based mechanism that differentiates children and adolescents with MDD from normal controls.*

There is general clinical consensus that the tricyclics are useful in treating depression in children and adolescents, but only one carefully controlled prospective clinical trial has demonstrated clear efficacy for using tricyclic antidepressants compared to a placebo. This relatively small scientific data base supporting the efficacy of the tricyclics for children and adolescents, compared to the substantial scientific data base supporting the efficacy of the tricyclics for adult-onset MDD, may be due to significant developmental and biological differences between childhood- and adolescent-onset MDD versus adult-onset MDD. Serotonergic agents such as fluoxetine also show promise in treating early-onset MDD. If it is ultimately demonstrated that these drugs are efficacious in early-onset MDD, this would support the role of the serotonergic system in childhood and adolescent MDD.

In summary, although the number of scientific studies on early-onset MDD is limited, the data accumulated so far support the hypothesis of an underlying biological mechanism probably involving dysregulation of one or more of the neurotransmitter systems in the brain.

Medical Management of MDD

Children and adolescents with MDD should be treated by a child psychiatrist with clinical expertise in this disease. The three main components of therapy are pharmacotherapy, family education, and psychotherapy.

Pharmacotherapy generally consists of one of the tricyclic antidepressants. There is broad clinical consensus that these agents are of some benefit in the management of MDD in children and adolescents. While the tricyclic antidepressants are widely used for depression in children and adolescents, only one clinical trial out of seven has shown these agents to be superior to a placebo. However, a dose-response relationship between the blood level of the antidepressant and clinical improvement has been established in prepubertal children with MDD; this strongly suggests that efficacious treatment may require both high dosages and appropriate blood levels of the tricyclics. In adolescents with MDD, no correlation has yet been found between clinical response and the blood level of the antidepressant. Any child or adolescent treated with a tricyclic antidepressant must be carefully monitored because of the potential for cardiac toxicity and other significant side effects. In adolescents who are refractory to tricyclic therapy, the addition of lithium or a switch to a monoamine oxidase inhibitor (MAOI) may be useful. Unfortunately, many adolescents may not be willing to adhere to the strict diet that must accompany the use of the MAOI. Finally, recent experience with fluoxetine suggests that this serotonergic agent may be useful in the management of MDD in early-onset depression. The main advantage of fluoxetine is that it lacks many of the side effects of the other antidepressants. But fluoxetine has not yet been established as efficacious in prospective randomized clinical trials for early-onset depression.

Family education is important because it helps the family understand and approach MDD as a chronic, recurrent illness. Such an approach improves compliance with treatment. Altering familial expectations has been shown to help reduce the rate of relapse and reduce the tensions of living with an adult with MDD, and it may be expected to do the same for children with MDD.

Psychotherapy should be aimed at ameliorating the interpersonal and social deficits associated with depressive symptomatology. Additionally, cognitive therapy can be aimed at correcting the cognitive distortions associated with the depressive state and may be effective in the treatment of MDD.

Research Directions

More research is needed to understand the underlying biological mechanisms of MDD in children and adolescents. An understanding of the exact nature of the dysregulation in neurotransmitters could lead to better pharmacological strategies in the treatment of this disorder. Well-designed prospective clinical trials using the newer antidepressant agents such as fluoxetine should be encouraged.

Reference

American Psychiatric Association. *Diagnostic and Statistical Manual of Mental Disorders.* (DSM-III-R.) Washington, D.C.: American Psychiatric Association, 1989.

Additional Sources

Ambrosini, P. J. "Pharmacotherapy in Child and Adolescent Major Depressive Disorder." In H. Y. Meltzer (ed.), *Psychopharmacology: The Third Generation of Progress.* New York: Raven Press, 1987.

Fleming, J. E., and Offord, D. R. "Epidemiology of Childhood Depressive Disorders: A Critical Review." *Journal of the American Academy of Child and Adolescent Psychiatry,* 1990, *29,* 571–580.

Jensen, J. B., and Garfinkel, B. D. "Growth Hormone Dysregulation in Children with Major Depressive Disorder." *Journal of the American Academy of Child and Adolescent Psychiatry,* 1990, 29 (2), 295–301.

Kutcher, S. P., Williamson, P., Silverberg, J., Marton, P., Malkin, D., and Malkin, A. "Nocturnal Growth Hormone Secretion in Depressed Older Adolescents." *Journal of the American Academy of Child and Adolescent Psychiatry,* 1988, 27 (6), 751–754.

Puig-Antich, J., Goetz, R., Davies, M., Fein, M., Hanlon, C., Chambers, W. J.,

Tabrizi, M. A., Sachar, E. J., and Weitzman, E. D. "Growth Hormone Secretion in Prepubertal Children with Major Depression, II: Sleep-Related Plasma Concentrations During a Depressive Episode." *Archives of General Psychiatry*, 1984, *41*, 463–466.

Puig-Antich, J., Goetz, D., Davies, M., Kaplan, T., Davies, S., Ostrow, L., Asnis, L., Twomey, J., Iyengar, S., and Ryan, N. D. "A Controlled Family History Study of Prepubertal Major Depressive Disorder." *Archives of General Psychiatry*, 1989, *46*, 406–418.

Puig-Antich, J., Novacenko, H., Davies, M., Chambers, W. J., Tabrizi, M. A., Krawiec, V., Ambrosini, P. J., and Sachar, E. J. "Growth Hormone Secretion in Prepubertal Children with Major Depression, I: Final Report on Response to Insulin-Induced Hypoglycemia During a Depressive Episode." *Archives of General Psychiatry*, 1984, *41*, 455–460.

Puig-Antich, J., Novacenko, H., Davies, M., Tabrizi, M. A., Ambrosini, P., Goetz, R., Bianca, J., Goetz, D., and Sachar, E. J. "Growth Hormone Secretion in Prepubertal Children with Major Depression, III: Response to Insulin-Induced Hypoglycemia after Recovery from a Depressive Episode and in a Drug-Free State." *Archives of General Psychiatry*, 1984, *41*, 471–475.

Ryan, N. D., and Puig-Antich, J. "Affective Illness in Adolescence." In A. J. Frances and R. E. Hales (eds.), *American Psychiatric Association Annual Review*. Vol. 5. Washington, D.C.: American Psychiatric Press, 1986.

Ryan, N. D., Puig-Antich, J., and Ambrosini, P. "The Clinical Picture of Major Depression in Children and Adolescents." *Archives of General Psychiatry*, 1987, *44*, 854–861.

Ryan, N. D., Puig-Antich, J., Rabinovich, H., Ambrosini, P., Robinson, D., Nelson, B., and Novacenko, H. "Growth Hormone Response to Desmethylimipramine in Depressed and Suicidal Adolescents." *Journal of Affective Disorders*, 1988, *15*, 323–337.

DAVID A. BRENT *is chief, Division of Child and Adolescent Psychiatry, and director, Services for Teens at Risk, Western Psychiatric Institute and Clinic, University of Pittsburgh School of Medicine.*

*The most commonly diagnosed behavioral disorder in childhood,
attention deficit hyperactivity disorder has a neurobiological and
genetic basis and is responsive to treatment.*

Attention Deficit Hyperactivity Disorder

*Lisa Amaya-Jackson, Richard H. Mesco,
James J. McGough, Dennis P. Cantwell*

Attention deficit hyperactivity disorder (ADHD) is the most commonly diagnosed behavioral disorder in childhood. Between 2 and 20 percent of all children are estimated to be affected. ADHD occurs from three to eight times more often in boys than in girls. ADHD's core symptoms are a triad of inattention, impulsivity, and hyperactivity. ADHD children do not "look before they leap." Restless and fidgety, they often interrupt conversations, call out in class, and cannot sit still. They have great difficulty following directions, completing assigned work on time, or completing tasks at all, especially if rewards are not immediately forthcoming. ADHD children generally lack the social skills appropriate to their age group. Often unpopular, they may hit other children without provocation and are frequently identified as the "class clown." At times, finding themselves caught in a situation they have unwittingly provoked, they will consciously act out with even more inappropriate behavior in an attempt to cover up the involuntary nature of their impulsive acts. Thus, they end up making a bad situation only worse.

At least 25 percent of children diagnosed with ADHD also suffer from a communication or learning disorder. Another 40 percent exhibit patterns of behavior that include starting fights, stealing, lying (conduct disorder), or persistent disobedience, defiance, and rule breaking (oppositional defiant disorder). Because most people still do not understand the biological factors underlying these behaviors, parents, teachers, coaches, and other adults often think that ADHD children are undisciplined, stupid, lazy, or simply bad. However, the overwhelming body of scientific evidence suggests that these children are suffering from a brain-based disorder that

NEW DIRECTIONS FOR MENTAL HEALTH SERVICES, no. 54, Summer 1992 © Jossey-Bass Publishers

is at least partly heritable and is responsive to medical and supportive intervention.

ADHD is usually diagnosed in childhood, when its symptoms first occur, but it persists through adolescence and adulthood in a significant number of cases. Research clearly shows that some of the long-term consequences of untreated ADHD include poor school performance, lifelong academic and occupational underachievement, development of low self-image and poor self-esteem, juvenile delinquency, higher rates of alcohol and substance abuse, and adult criminality.

Historical View of ADHD

A hundred years ago, the psychologist William James noted that the inability to sustain attention seemed related to poor control and impulsive behavior; he suggested a single neurological deficiency as the underlying cause. Today, studies performed with the positron emission tomography (PET) scanner suggest that James may have been correct.

The great influenza epidemic of 1917–18 left many people with serious neurological impairments, the aftereffects of the damage done by the flu virus and the fever it had caused. Work with one such group that had suffered decreased physical ability eventually led to the development of effective treatments for Parkinsonism. A different group suffered from an almost opposite set of aftereffects, including increased motor activity, impulsivity, and inattention: the neurological symptom triad of ADHD. The term *postencephalitic behavior disorder* was applied to these individuals, who seem to have suffered from a form of ADHD.

Recognition of this syndrome led to later observations of hyperactivity unrelated to the flu epidemic. Clinicians in the 1930s coined terms like *organic driveness* and *restlessness syndrome* for this symptom complex. In the 1940s and 1950s, research on behavioral effects of experimental injuries to monkeys' brains implicated damage to forebrain structures as a possible cause for such behavior disorders in humans. This was labeled *minimal brain damage;* it signified gross structural injury to the brain. By the 1960s, MBD came to stand for *minimal brain dysfunction,* in keeping with a more physiological understanding of the disorder.

When both psychoanalytic and behavioral theorists were constructing models that often blamed parents for various developmental and behavioral disorders, including MBD, other researchers began to look separately at the different aspects of MBD and its possible underlying causes. *Hyperactivity* (then called *hyperkinetic reaction of childhood*), *dyslexia,* and *learning disability* all entered the vocabulary as a more sophisticated understanding of the complex interactions between biological and environmental factors began to emerge. In the 1980s, the diagnostic term *attention deficit disorder* came into use; it could be specified further as "with or without hyperactivity." At present, the newer term *attention deficit hyperactivity disorder (ADHD)* incorporates both facets of the disorder.

The current description of ADHD as a constellation of symptoms and behaviors characterized by inattention, impulsivity, and hyperactivity is very similar to the observations made by William James in 1890. The most significant changes have come with recent research, from which a somewhat consistent picture of the neurobiological basis of ADHD can begin to be drawn.

Neurotransmitter Studies

Several neurotransmitters—chemicals that send signals from one brain cell (neuron) to another—have been implicated in the development of ADHD: among them, serotonin, dopamine, adrenaline, and noradrenaline. All may play a part in ADHD, some more than others in one child as compared to another.

The most compelling evidence implicates deficiencies in neural pathways using dopamine as the most important neurotransmitter defect underlying ADHD. Dopamine is found in high concentrations in the structures of the frontal and prefrontal cortex—brain areas known to determine control over social behavior, especially by inhibiting inappropriate behavior. Brain electrical studies have shown that activity in the prefrontal area signals the onset of even the simplest voluntary movement. Several different indirect biochemical studies have consistently shown that hyperactive children have low overall levels of dopamine. Dopamine is also the main neurotransmitter in the striate cortex, a part of the brain essential for normal motor movement. At least 50 percent of children with the neurological movement disorder Tourette's syndrome (TS) (see Chapter Four) also have a diagnosis of ADHD. There is likewise a higher rate of tics and movement disorders in children with ADHD, evidence suggesting a biological connection between the two disorders. Medications that alter the activity of dopamine pathways, though in different ways, are the treatment mainstays for TS and ADHD.

Medication and Dietary Factors

The medical treatment of ADHD is the single most extensively studied area of child psychopharmacology, spanning over three decades. All the medications used successfully to treat ADHD affect the dopamine and noradrenaline systems. These include stimulants such as methylphenidate (Ritalin), dextroamphetamine (Dexedrine), and pemoline (Cylert), and heterocyclics like imipramine (Tofranil). Proper pharmacological therapy has often been shown to improve school performance, significantly enhance the quality of the child's interaction in the family, and decrease the incidence of aggressive behavior.

It was suggested in the 1960s and 1970s that food additives might play a causal role in behavior disorders; the Feingold diet is the best known outgrowth of this never-proven theory. When every scientific study failed to indicate any significant association between food additives and hyperactivity, sugar was next suggested as a causative factor. To date, no scientific studies have delineated any consistent causal link between dietary factors and the diagnosis of ADHD.

Genetic and Developmental Factors

There is strong evidence for the heritability of ADHD. Some early twin studies showed a 100 percent concordance rate for ADHD in identical twins. Studies that used larger sample sizes and included children with only *some* symptoms of ADHD, as opposed to the full disorder, show the concordance of symptoms in identical twins to be greater than 50 percent, compared with 33 percent in fraternal twins. In other family studies, from 20 to 33 percent of the parents and siblings of children with ADHD have been found to have sufficient symptoms to warrant a diagnosis of ADHD.

Environmental factors that have been associated with the development of ADHD include exposure in utero to such toxins as alcohol, cocaine, nicotine from maternal smoking or passive inhalation, hypoxic insult during birth, and low birth weight. In ADHD children there is an increased incidence of minor physical anomalies such as widely spaced eyes, abnormal eye folds, low-set ears, and unbroken palmar creases. Based on the available research, current estimates are that ADHD traits are from 30 to 50 percent genetic and about 30 percent environmentally induced.

Brain Imaging Studies

The most recent and elegant evidence supporting the view of ADHD as the behavioral expression of one or more specific underlying disorders of brain functioning comes from PET scan studies. These have shown that overall brain metabolism is 8 percent lower in adults who have been hyperactive since childhood but have never been treated with medication than in nonhyperactive adults. Of sixty identified brain areas studied in the hyperactive adults, thirty areas had lower metabolic rates, and no area had a rate that was significantly higher. Areas that showed particularly low rates of activity included the prefrontal and premotor cortex (which modulate attention, social judgment, and movement), left temporal and left parietal cortex (language and communication), somatosensory cortex (body awareness), and other areas around the Rolandic Fissure.

This is the most powerful, direct evidence to date in support of underarousal of the brain as the general underlying mechanism of the constellation of ADHD and its associated behaviors. The PET studies are consistent with the observed therapeutic effects of stimulant medication, the higher rates of learning and communication disorders seen with ADHD, and data from neuropsychological testing. As a whole, a coherent picture of ADHD emerges as a set of behaviors stemming from a biological disorder of the brain.

Management of ADHD

Assessment and treatment of the ADHD child must take into account the biological, psychological, social, developmental, and educational aspects of the disorder. Reports from parents and teachers about the child's performance in different settings are a necessary complement to the standard psychiatric clinical history, observation, and interviews. Rating scales and other structured instruments can help provide a more objective comparison of a child with his or her peers and can also assist in monitoring the therapeutic effectiveness of any intervention.

The diagnosis of ADHD does not automatically require that a child be placed on medications, yet stimulants are often a highly effective and generally safe method of treatment. About two-thirds of ADHD children will demonstrate a positive therapeutic response. When stimulants are not helpful or are medically contraindicated, antidepressants and other medications have been used successfully. Benefit is seen in the form of less disruptive classroom behavior, decreased aggression, better concentration, improved productivity and accuracy of work, and better compliance with requests from responsible adults. Improvement can be noted by means of parent and teacher rating scales and on laboratory measures such as the Continuous Performance Task and the Paired Associate Learning Task.

Because a substantial group of ADHD children are academic under-achievers, and because many of them suffer from specific learning or communication disorders, formal educational testing and a general screening evaluation of speech and language should be performed. Often, these services can be provided by the school, if the parent requests in writing that an individualized educational plan be developed for a child. The results of such testing will help determine which classroom strategies, special resources, or class placement will be optimal for a given student. ADHD children generally fare best in smaller, highly structured settings.

One means of addressing the cognitive deficits of ADHD children is through social skills groups aimed at improving peer relationships. Another way is to teach the child self-monitoring skills, as in the "Stop, Listen, Look, Think" approach. There is little evidence that dynamic psychotherapy is efficacious for these children. In cases where oppositional and conduct disorders are a problem, behavioral modification strategies such as the use of praise and reinforcement, "time out," sticker charts, and point systems can be implemented at school and at home. Parent training and counseling can help parents learn these different behavioral strategies to work with their child's problematical behavior and to alter situational variables so that power struggles can be avoided. Consistent, specific techniques are a particularly useful means for reducing conflict in the home and in effecting behavioral change in the ADHD child.

Cooperation and collaboration among the clinician, school personnel, and the family are the keys to a comprehensive, successful treatment strategy for the ADHD child. Parents' support, education, and advocacy groups like the National Alliance for the Mentally Ill Children and Adolescents Network (NAMI CAN) and Children with Attention Deficit Disorder (CH.A.D.D.) can help families who find comfort in sharing insights with other caring families in similar circumstances. Drawing on the combined wisdom of others can help lessen the family's and the child's sense of stigma, help the family and the child cope with the stresses caused by the child's brain disorder and society's reaction to it, and assist families in obtaining optimal resources available for the child.

Additional Sources

Barkley, R. A. *Attention Deficit Hyperactivity Disorder: A Handbook for Diagnosis and Treatment*. New York: Guilford Press, 1990.

Cantwell, D. P., and Hanna, G. L. "Attention Deficit Hyperactivity Disorder." In *Eighth Annual Review of Psychiatry 1989*. Washington, D.C.: American Psychiatric Press, 1990.

Zametkin, A. J., Nordahl, T. E., Gross, M., King, A. C., Semple, W. E., Rumsey, J., Hamburger, S., and Cohen, R. M. "Cerebral Glucose Metabolism in Adults with Hyperactivity of Childhood Onset." *New England Journal of Medicine*, 1990, 323 (20), 1361–1366.

LISA AMAYA-JACKSON *is a Robert Wood Johnson Clinical Scholar in Research and Child Psychiatry at the University of North Carolina School of Medicine in Chapel Hill.*

RICHARD H. MESCO *is assistant professor of psychiatry, University of New Mexico School of Medicine, and is an attending child and adolescent psychiatrist at Children's Psychiatric Hospital in Albuquerque, New Mexico.*

JAMES J. MCGOUGH *is assistant clinical professor of child psychiatry at UCLA Neuropsychiatric Institute and is in private practice in Los Angeles.*

DENNIS P. CANTWELL *is Joseph Campbell Professor of Child Psychiatry and director of residency training in child psychiatry at the UCLA Neuropsychiatric Institute.*

Disruptive behavior disorders comprise a category of behavioral disorders with common clinical, and possibly biological, characteristics.

Biological Correlates of Impulsive Disruptive Behavior Disorders: Attention Deficit Hyperactivity Disorder, Conduct Disorder, and Borderline Personality Disorder

Josephine Elia, David M. Stoff, Emil F. Coccaro

Attention deficit hyperactivity disorder (ADHD), conduct disorder (CD), and borderline personality disorder (BPD) are heterogeneous behavioral disorders of unknown etiology that share some common characteristic symptoms.

Clinical Description

ADHD and CD usually become evident in childhood and, along with oppositional defiant disorder, constitute the category of disruptive behavior disorders (DBD), which accounts for most referrals to child psychiatry clinics. BPD, relatively well characterized in adults, is only now beginning to be studied in children.

Impulsive disruptive behavior disorders often occur in combination. ADHD and CD have been found to occur together in 30 to 50 percent of cases (Biederman, Newcorn, and Sprich, 1991). In addition, a subgroup of patients with BPD simultaneously meeting criteria for ADHD has been identified in adults (Andrulonis, Glueck, Stroebel, and Vogel, 1982). Among these disorders, there is considerable comorbidity with mood disorders, anxiety disorders, learning disabilities, mental retardation, and Tourette's syndrome (Biederman, Newcorn, and Sprich, 1991).

ADHD. ADHD is characterized by varying degrees of inattention, impulsiveness, and hyperactivity. (See Chapter Seven.) Schoolchildren with ADHD are vulnerable to later antisocial behavior and to continued impulsiveness and educational failure. Males with ADHD as children are ten times more likely to show diagnostic features of ADHD at follow-up (Gittelman, Mannuzza, Shenker, and Bonagura, 1985). The persistence of ADHD appears to be a good predictor of whether conduct problems develop in later adult life.

Comorbidity of ADHD with other behavioral disorders may influence outcome at follow-up. Children with ADHD plus CD may have more serious clinical courses and poorer outcomes than children with ADHD without CD, according to some (Farrington, Loeber, and Van Kammen, 1989) but not all studies (Hechtman, Weiss, Perlman, and Amsel, 1984). This suggests that ADHD's course is influenced by multiple rather than single factors. For example, aggressive behavior in children and familial factors tend to predict future antisocial behavior more strongly than does a history of ADHD.

CD. Children with CD persistently disregard rules and violate others' rights. (See Chapter Nine.) Onset is usually prepubertal in boys and postpubertal in girls. These children frequently initiate fights, deliberately destroy property, and may confront a victim in order to steal. Covert stealing is common. Often youngsters are truant from school and may run away from home. Drug or alcohol abuse is frequently present; sexual activity often begins early. Self-esteem is low and often hidden under the "tough" image. Poor frustration tolerance, irritability, temper outbursts, anxiety, and depression are frequently seen. Academically, reading and other verbal skills are usually below grade level. Attentional difficulties, impulsivity, and hyperactivity are also common.

Conduct disorders constitute a heterogeneous group of problems. The largest subgroup of patients is made up of children with comorbid ADHD. The association between major depression and disruptive behaviors has been commonly observed in clinic populations: one-third of the boys meeting criteria for depression also met criteria for CD in one study. Improvement in depressed mood by imipramine treatment was followed by a decrease in disruptive behavior in the majority of children (Puig-Antich, 1982). But epidemiological studies will be needed to clarify whether major depression and CD are truly associated in children.

BPD. A DSM-III-R diagnosis (American Psychiatric Association, 1987) only given to adults at this time, BPD usually begins by early adulthood and is characterized by pervasive instability of interpersonal relationships, mood, and self-image.[1] Historically, the two categories of disorders using the term *borderline* in children include the schizotypal personality disorder/ autism/schizophrenia spectrum and the borderline personality disorder spectrum. Since schizotypal personality disorder, autism, and childhood schizophrenia have become more clearly defined with distinct criteria, the term *borderline* is no longer appropriate and should only be used in reference to BPD.

Several researchers have been trying to investigate possible diagnostic criteria derived from reported clinical symptoms in order to obtain a consensus regarding the diagnosis of BPD in children. Vela, Gottlieb, and Gottlieb (1983) clustered behaviors in six symptom groups: (1) disturbed interpersonal relationships, (2) disturbances in the sense of reality, (3) excessive intense anxiety, (4) impulsive behavior, (5) fleeting "neurotic-like" symptoms, and (6) uneven or distorted development. Bemporad and Cichetti (1982) developed an overlapping set of diagnostic criteria describing the psychopathology of "BPD" within the following areas: (1) relationships to others, (2) thought content and process, (3) nature and extent of anxiety, (4) lack of control, (5) fluctuations in functioning, and (6) poor social functioning (including inability to learn from past experience or adapt to novel situations, and poor hygiene). While the validity of the Vela criteria has not been investigated, the Bemporad criteria have been found to lack diagnostic "specificity"—that is, these criteria did not distinguish children with "BPD" from "non-BPD" children (Gualtieri and Van Bourgondien, 1987). "BPD" diagnoses by DSM-III criteria may also be without strong validity. Unfortunately, validity for the "BPD" diagnosis in children and adolescents from longitudinal follow-up studies is not available, even though most clinicians seem to assume that these children grow into borderline adults. In contrast to a categorical diagnosis of personality disorders such as BPD, there is better support for the validity of the three main personality disorder clusters—that is, "dimensions" of personality pathology (Brent, Zelnick, Bukstein, and Brown, 1990). This suggests that a dimensional approach to personality pathology in children and adolescents, as in adults, may be a fruitful approach to understanding certain types of behaviors.

Pathophysiological Studies

A growing body of diverse pathophysiological data supports the conclusion that there is an underlying neurobiological basis for ADHD, CD, and BPD in children and adolescents.

ADHD. Animal models relevant to ADHD have suggested that a deficiency in catecholamine neurotransmitters (dopamine, norepinephrine) may have etiological relevance for ADHD. In one PET study, cerebral metabolism of glucose was lower in adults who had both a childhood history of hyperactivity and an offspring with ADHD (Zametkin and others, 1990). Among the brain areas examined, the greatest reduction in cerebral glucose metabolism was found in the premotor cortex and the superior prefrontal cortex. These findings cannot be interpreted as characteristic of ADHD. Further studies must be done comparing this population to people with other psychiatric disorders in which an impairment of attention also occurs.

CD. In adults, impulsive-aggressive behavior has been associated with reduced cerebrospinal fluid concentrations of the serotonin metabolite 5-hydroxyindolacetic acid (CSF 5-HIAA), considered to be a measure of brain serotonin activity (Brown and Goodwin, 1986). And a reduction was found in neuroendocrine responses to fenfluramine (a releaser of brain serotonin) challenge in adults who had personality disorders with significant clinical histories of impulsive-aggressive behavior. This suggests reduced overall brain serotonin function in persons with impulsive-aggressive behaviors (Coccaro and others, 1989). Both fenfluramine challenge and CSF 5-HIAA studies demonstrate an inverse relationship between impulsive-aggressive behaviors and brain serotonin function in adults. Because there is evidence that measures of both impulsive aggression and brain serotonin function may be correlated within individuals over time, it is possible that the same relationships may be present in children and adolescents. While studies in these areas are just beginning, reduced CSF 5-HIAA concentrations have been reported in children and adolescents with disruptive behavior disorders compared to age-, sex-, and race-matched children with obsessive-compulsive disorder (Kruesi and others, 1990).

Less invasive measures have also been investigated in patients with CD. Given the fact that platelets share many characteristics with brain cells, studies involving platelets may yield important information about brain function. There has been some question regarding the validity of this premise (Stoff and others, 1991a). Specifically, we have found that platelet imipramine binding, a possible measure of brain serotonin function, was reduced in patients with CD in one study (Stoff and others, 1987) but not in another (Stoff and others, 1991b). On the other hand, platelet monoamine oxidase (MAO), the enzyme that metabolizes monoamine neurotransmitters (serotonin, norepinephrine, dopamine), was correlated with impulsivity in patients with disruptive behavior disorders (Stoff and others, 1989). This finding is consistent with the serotonergic hypothesis of impulsive aggression as seen in adults, and with the findings that treatment with MAO inhibitors is effective in children with ADHD.

Finally, urinary free cortisol (UFC) levels have been reported lower in adults with disruptive behavior disorders (Virkkunen, 1985). In a group of habitually violent antisocial men compared to other types of offenders and controls, Virkkunen (1985) found lower UFC levels in the violent men. But Kruesi and others (1989) did not find any difference in UFC output between a group of nineteen boys with attention deficit or CD or both and normal controls.

BPD. Results from varied reports of biological correlates showing EEG abnormalities, enzyme deficiencies, and neurotransmitter variances in "borderline" children must be interpreted cautiously. As stated before, the subjects in these studies met different diagnostic criteria sets for "BPD." Reports of recent studies must also be interpreted cautiously; even though clinical description of "BPD" is becoming more clearly defined, validity in children remains to be established. Yet data from adults with "BPD" suggest that these patients may have reduced brain serotonin function (Coccaro and others, 1989). While evidence for reduced brain serotonin function appeared to be specific for the "BPD" diagnosis, closer examination of the data revealed that this finding was more basically due to the fact that "BPD" patients are particularly impulsive and aggressive. This suggested that a behavioral dimension of impulsive aggression, also noted in children and adolescents with CD, is more clearly responsible for this relationship between categorical diagnosis and a measure of brain serotonin function.

Medical Management

The treatment of these disorders is multidisciplinary. Stimulant agents such as methylphenidate, dextroamphetamine, and pemoline have been consistently proven effective in reducing ADHD symptoms. Children with ADHD alone, or ADHD with CD, or ADHD with oppositional defiant disorder have been found to respond.

Antidepressants should be used as second-line drugs when stimulants cannot be used because of adverse effects. Antidepressants may also be useful in cases where depression is a significant factor and in children with Tourette's syndrome, where tics may be exacerbated by stimulants.

In addition, lithium is being explored in children with impulsive-aggressive outbursts (Campbell and others, 1984). Preliminary data in adults that serotonin-type drugs (for example, fluoxetine) may be effective in reducing impulsive aggression (Coccaro, Astill, Herbert, and Schut, 1990) suggest that such drugs may be considered in the future for children after research on adults is completed. Along with pharmacotherapy, behavioral management systems are essential. These should focus on providing structure, well-defined limits, unquestionable behavioral expectation, and positive tangible and intangible rewards. Working closely with schools is essential. Promoting success in academics, socialization, and behavior is invaluable. A closed loop should be formed between the parents-teacher-physician to ensure that the child functions maximally.

Research Directions

At this time, diagnosis of disruptive behavior disorder in children rests on clinical assessment. There are as yet no laboratory tests, brain imaging studies, or neuropsychological evaluation procedures that can distinguish one diagnostic group from another. But sufficient evidence from biological studies in adults and preliminary studies in children supports a neurobiological basis for these disorders in children. With the identification of specific biological abnormalities, biologically based treatments that can ameliorate these abnormalities and hence normalize these disruptive behaviors may be developed. Research in this area needs to include investigations related to the genetic and familial vulnerabilities associated with these disorders. Considerable research needs to be done to identify the genetic influences that increase the likelihood of the occurrence of these disorders. Also, environmental factors, prenatal and postnatal insults, and socioeconomic variables interact in a complex way with these biogenetic influences. Recent developments in brain imaging using MRI and PET scans may provide noninvasive methods of examining brain structure and metabolic activity.

Note

1. Although BPD is "officially" a DSM-III-R diagnosis of adulthood (American Psychiatric Association, 1987), clinicians in some treatment settings diagnose this condition in adolescence. This information is provided for the sake of those adolescents and their families.

References

American Psychiatric Association. *Diagnostic and Statistical Manual of Mental Disorders.* (DSM-III-R.) Washington, D.C.: American Psychiatric Association, 1987.

Andrulonis, P. A., Glueck, B. C., Stroebel, C. F., and Vogel, N. G. "Borderline Personality Subcategories." *Journal of Nervous and Mental Disease,* 1982, *170,* 670–679.

Bemporad, J. R., and Cichetti, D. "Borderline Syndromes in Childhood: Criteria for Diagnosis." *American Journal of Psychiatry,* 1982, *139,* 596–601.

Biederman, J., Newcorn, J., and Sprich, S. "Comorbidity of Attention Deficit Hyperactivity Disorder with Conduct, Depressive, Anxiety, and Other Disorders." *American Journal of Psychiatry,* 1991, *148,* 564–577.

Brent, D. A., Zelnick, J. P., Bukstein, O., and Brown, R. V. "Reliability and Validity of the Structured Interview for Personality Disorders in Adolescents." *Journal of the American Academy of Child and Adolescent Psychiatry,* 1990, *29,* 349.

Brown, G. L., and Goodwin, F. K. "Human Aggression: A Biological Perspective." In W. H. Reid, D. Dorr, J. D. Walker, and J. W. Bonner (eds.), *Unmasking the Psychopath—Antisocial Personality and Related Syndromes.* New York: Norton, 1986.

Campbell, M., Small, A. M., Green, W. H., Jennings, S. J., Perry, R., Bennett, W. G., and Anderson, L. "Behavioral Efficacy of Haloperidol and Lithium Carbonate: A Comparison in Hospitalized Aggressive Children with Conduct Disorder." *Archives of General Psychiatry,* 1984, *41,* 650–656.

Coccaro, E. F., Astill, J. L., Herbert, J., and Schut, A. "Fluoxetine Treatment of Impulsive Aggression in DSM-III-R Personality Disorder Patients." *Journal of Clinical Psychopharmacology,* 1990, *10,* 373–375.

Coccaro, E. F., Siever, L. J., Klar, H. M., Maurer, G., Cochrane, K., Cooper, T. B., Mohs, R. C., and Davis, K. L. "Serotonergic Studies in Patients with Affective and Personality Disorders: Correlates with Suicidal and Impulsive Aggressive Behavior." *Archives of General Psychiatry,* 1989, *46,* 587–599.

Farrington, D. P., Loeber, R., and Van Kammen, D. P. "Long-Term Criminal Outcomes of Hyperactivity–Impulsivity–Attention Deficit and Conduct Problems in Childhood." In

L. N. Robins and M. R. Rutter (eds.), *Straight and Devious Pathways to Adulthood.* New York: Cambridge University Press, 1989.

Gittelman, R., Mannuzza, S., Shenker, R., and Bonagura, N. "Hyperactive Boys Almost Grown Up, I: Psychiatric Status." *Archives of General Psychiatry,* 1985, *42,* 937–947.

Gualtieri, C. T., and Van Bourgondien, M. E. "So-Called Borderline Children." *American Journal of Psychiatry,* 1987, *144,* 832.

Hechtman, L., Weiss, G., Perlman, T., and Amsel, R. "Hyperactives as Young Adults: Initial Predictors of Adult Outcome." *Journal of the American Academy of Child Psychiatry,* 1984, *23,* 250–260.

Kruesi, M.J.P., Rapoport, J. L., Hamburger, S., Hibbs, E., Potter, W. Z., Lenane, M., and Brown, G. L. "Cerebrospinal Fluid Monoamine Metabolites, Aggression, and Impulsivity in Disruptive Behavior Disorders of Children and Adolescents." *Archives of General Psychiatry,* 1990, *47,* 419–426.

Kruesi, M.J.P., Schmidt, M. E., Donnelly, M., Hibbs, E. D., and Hamburger, S. D. "Urinary Free Cortisol Output and Disruptive Behavior in Children." *Journal of the American Academy of Child and Adolescent Psychiatry,* 1989, *28* (3), 441–443.

Puig-Antich, J. "Major Depression and Conduct Disorder in Prepuberty." *Journal of the American Academy of Child and Adolescent Psychiatry,* 1982, *21,* 118–128.

Stoff, D. M., Friedman, E., Pollock, L., Vitiello, B., Kendall, P., and Bridger, W. H. "Elevated Platelet MAO Is Related to Impulsivity in Disruptive Behavioral Disorders." *Journal of the American Academy of Child and Adolescent Psychiatry,* 1989, *28,* 754–760.

Stoff, D. M., Goldman, W., Bridger, W. H., Jain, A. K., and Pylypiw, A. "No Correlation Between Platelet Imipramine Binding and CSF 5-HIAA in Neurosurgical Patients." *Psychiatry Research,* 1991a, *33,* 323–326.

Stoff, D. M., Ieni, J., Friedman, E., Bridger, W. H., Pollock, L., and Vitiello, B. "Platelet (^{3}H)-Imipramine Binding, Serotonin Uptake, and Plasma Alpha-1 Acid Glycoprotein in Disruptive Disorders." *Biological Psychiatry,* 1991b, *29,* 494–498.

Stoff, D. M., Pollock, L., Vitiello, B., Behar, D., and Bridger, W. H. "Reduction of (^{3}H)-Imipramine Binding Sites on Platelets of Conduct-Disordered Children." *Neuropsychopharmacology,* 1987, *1,* 55–62.

Vela, R., Gottlieb, E. H., and Gottlieb, H. P. "Borderline Syndromes in Childhood: A Critical Review." In K. S. Robson (ed.), *The Borderline Child.* New York: McGraw-Hill, 1983.

Virkkunen, M. "Urinary Free Cortisol Excretion in Habitually Violent Offenders." *Acta Psychiatrica Scandinavia,* 1985, *72,* 40–44.

Zametkin, A. J., Nordahl, T. E., Gross, M., King, A. C., Semple, W. E., Rumsey, J., Hamburger, S., and Cohen, R. M. "Cerebral Glucose Metabolism in Adults with Hyperactivity of Childhood Onset." *New England Journal of Medicine,* 1990, *323,* 1361–1366.

JOSEPHINE ELIA *is director of child psychiatry at St. Christopher's Hospital, Department of Psychiatry, Medical College of Pennsylvania.*

DAVID M. STOFF *is director of behavioral pharmacology, Division of Child Psychiatry, Department of Psychiatry, Medical College of Pennsylvania at the Eastern Pennsylvania Psychiatric Institute.*

EMIL F. COCCARO *is director of the Clinical Neuroscience Research Unit, Department of Psychiatry, Medical College of Pennsylvania at the Eastern Pennsylvania Psychiatric Institute.*

Conduct disorder is one of the most common disorders in children and adolescents, and yet we know little about its cause and treatment.

Pharmacological Treatment of Conduct Disorder

Arthur Rifkin

Conduct disorder (CD) is a persistent pattern of behavior that violates the community's norms especially concerning aggression and trustworthiness. By persistent, we mean lasting at least six months. Brief or episodic misconduct is not included here and is of much less significance. The most common kinds of misconduct are stealing, running away, lying, fire setting, truancy from school or work, breaking into cars or buildings, deliberate destruction of property, cruelty to animals, forced sexual activity, using a weapon in fights, frequently initiating fights, stealing with confrontation (such as mugging, purse snatching, extortion, armed robbery), and physical cruelty to people. This list is ranked so that the symptoms mentioned first are more common (American Psychiatric Association, 1987).

There are two major types of conduct disorder. The group type is more common: the child usually misbehaves when in a peer group, for example in a gang. The other type is called solitary aggressive: the child usually initiates the misbehavior alone and is not part of a group. Some children show both types.

The most difficult part of making the diagnosis is delimiting the threshold between normal misbehavior and CD. Normal children often misbehave, and so it is impossible to define the threshold precisely. When the misbehavior definitely interferes with the child's adjustment at home, school, or elsewhere or is well beyond normal, even if the misbehavior does not hinder functioning very much, the diagnosis is clear. We must avoid judging these children as merely "bad" and deserving condemnation and punishment. Certainly, reasonable, consistent discipline is important, but making moral judgments does not help us understand or help children with CD.

NEW DIRECTIONS FOR MENTAL HEALTH SERVICES, no. 54, Summer 1992 ©Jossey-Bass Publishers

Hyperactivity, now known as attention deficit hyperactivity disorder (ADHD), may resemble CD, and the two often coexist. Children with ADHD who fidget, often interrupt, and cannot wait their turn are often considered to have a primary behavior problem. These children are often scolded, which leads them to respond with anger or pouting. But these behaviors do not persistently include the more serious aggressive antisocial behaviors present in CD.

A massive community survey done in Ontario, Canada, established the prevalence of both CD and ADHD. Children age four to sixteen from 1,869 households were evaluated. CD was found in 8.1 percent of the boys and 2.7 percent of the girls; 8.9 percent of the boys and 3.3 percent of the girls had ADHD (Boyle and others, 1987). Gittelman and co-workers (1985) examined 100 children an average of nine years after they had been diagnosed with ADHD; 40 percent still had ADHD and 27 percent also had CD. This shows how closely these disorders are connected.

CD must also be differentiated from specific developmental disorders in which children have difficulty with certain academic, language, speech, or motor skills. Such children may become frustrated by their poor performance and show anger and resentment, yet not to the extent described for CD. It is very important to distinguish these conditions from CD because treatments are different.

Pharmacological Treatment of CD

The first important point in the pharmacological management of CD is that if ADHD is also present, the ADHD should be adequately treated with stimulants *before* an attempt is made to treat the CD. The evidence that stimulants are effective in treating ADHD is overwhelming. Because ADHD symptoms may exacerbate coexisting CD, the ADHD should be treated first. If significant CD symptoms remain after initiating therapy for ADHD, drug therapy for CD should be considered.

Early studies on the pharmacological treatment of CD included the use of (1) stimulants (Arnold and others, 1976; Conners and others, 1971; Eisenberg and others, 1963), (2) neuroleptics (Barker and Fraser, 1968; Cunningham, Pillai, and Rogers, 1968; Goldberg and Kurland, 1974), and (3) anticonvulsants (Lefkowitz, 1969; Looker and Conners, 1970). None of these studies was able to establish the efficacy of any of these drug groups for CD.

More recently, two major groups of drugs have been investigated for the treatment of CD: the neuroleptics and lithium. The neuroleptics are often used to control agitation or violence in both children and adults, even in many nonpsychotic disorders. The short-term use of the neuroleptics for control of agitation or violence is well established, but the long-term efficacy of these drugs to control agitation or violence has not been established. Several studies demonstrated that lithium was effective in reducing aggressive behavior in adult males (Sheard, Marini, Bridges, and Wagner, 1976; Tupin and others, 1973). These studies led to the hypothesis that lithium might also be useful in children and adolescents with CD. Lithium has the advantage of being well tolerated by children; it also has fewer side effects than the neuroleptics.

The most important study on the medical treatment of CD has been by Campbell and others (1984), who treated sixty-one hospitalized children, age five to thirteen, with three different treatment arms: haloperidol (a neuroleptic), lithium, and a placebo. This study demonstrated that both haloperidol and lithium were clearly superior to a placebo in terms of reducing CD symptoms. The children on haloperidol had more side effects (mainly excessive sedation and muscle spasms) than the children on lithium. Therefore, the authors concluded that lithium was effective therapy for CD and had fewer side effects than a neuroleptic. These investigators then repeated their study (Campbell and Small, 1990), this time comparing lithium to a placebo. They again concluded that lithium was effective in treating CD. Thus, these important studies have concluded that lithium, a drug commonly used to treat bipolar disorder effectively in adults, is also effective in treating children with CD. But the Campbell studies (1984, 1990) have some shortcomings: (1) It is not clear if patients with ADHD alone were excluded. (2) It is not specified if some patients with CD in these studies had coexisting ADHD. Further research is needed to determine if lithium will be clearly effective in children with CD alone, without any component of ADHD. Because such a high proportion of children with CD also have ADHD, it will be important to compare lithium to a stimulant. Such studies are now underway, and a clearer picture of using lithium to treat CD should emerge in the next few years.

CD is particularly difficult to tolerate in adolescents, who, because of their greater maturity and size, can do more harm to others and to property than can young children. A two-week study of hospitalized adolescents with CD was performed comparing lithium to a placebo. None of the patients had coexisting ADHD or a previous history of ADHD (Rifkin, Karajgi, Boppana, and Pearl, 1989). There was no evidence that lithium was effective for the two-week trial period. It is possible that a longer study may have demonstrated a positive effect for lithium.

More research is needed to provide a more definitive answer to the question of which drug therapies are effective for CD. My present recommendation is the following: (1) Assess the patient for coexisting ADHD. (2) If there is evidence of ADHD, treat the patient with a stimulant. (3) If CD symptoms continue, or there is no evidence for ADHD, a lithium trial should be considered.

Future Directions

Further research is essential to study the possible efficacy of lithium in the medical treatment of CD. New imaging techniques—including computerized tomography (CT), magnetic resonance imaging (MRI), and positron emission tomography (PET) scanning—are adding new dimensions to the study of brain disorders. These new technologies should be applied to the systematic study of CD.

The finding that lithium, an effective drug for treating BD in adults, may possibly be effective in treating childhood CD suggests two things: (1) The discovery of lithium's mechanism of action could lead to an understanding of the biochemical nature of some patients with CD. (2) There may be an underlying biochemical relationship between bipolar disorder in adults and CD in children and adolescents. Unfortunately, there is no scientific evidence to support either of these speculations. Also, lithium has mild effects on several neurotransmitter systems such as norepinephrine and serotonin. But it is not clear how these effects are related to CD. Further scientific research is needed to define the underlying biochemical nature of CD.

References

American Psychiatric Association. *Diagnostic and Statistical Manual of Mental Disorders.* (DSM-III-R.) Washington, D.C.: American Psychiatric Association, 1987.

Arnold, L. E., Huestis, R. D., Smeltzer, D. J., Scheib, J., Wemmer, D., and Colner, G. "Levoamphetamine vs. Dextroamphetamine in Minimal Brain Dysfunction: Replication, Time Response, and Differential Effect by Diagnostic Group and Family Rating." *Archives of General Psychiatry,* 1976, *33,* 292–301.

Barker, P., and Fraser, I. "A Controlled Trial of Haloperidol in Children." *British Journal of Psychiatry,* 1968, *114,* 855–857.

Boyle, M. H., Offord, D. R., Hofmann, H. G., Catlin, J. A., Byles, J. A., Cadman, D. T., Crawford, J. M., Links, P. S., Rae-Grant, N. I., and Szatmari, P. "Ontario Child Health Study, II: Six-Month Prevalence of Disorders and Rates of Service Utilization." *Archives of General Psychiatry,* 1987, *44,* 832–836.

Campbell, M., and Small, A. M. "Lithium Carbonate in the Treatment of Hospitalized Children with Conduct Disorder." Paper presented at the 30th meeting of the New Drug Clinical Evaluation Units, National Institute of Mental Health, Key Biscayne, Fla., May 1990.

Campbell, M., Small, A. M., Green, W. H., Jennings, S. J., Perry, R., Bennett, W. G., and Anderson, L. "Behavioral Efficacy of Haloperidol and Lithium Carbonate." *Archives of General Psychiatry,* 1984, *41,* 650–658.

Conners, C. K., Kramer, R., Rothschild, G. H., Schwartz, L., and Stone, A. "Treatment of Young Delinquent Boys with Diphenylhydantoin Sodium and Methylphenidate: A Controlled Comparison." *Archives of General Psychiatry,* 1971, *24,* 156–160.

Cunningham, M. A., Pillai, V., and Rogers, W. J. "Haloperidol in the Treatment of Children with Severe Behavior Disorders." *British Journal of Psychiatry,* 1968, *114,* 845–854.

Eisenberg, L., Lachman, R., Molling, P. A., Lockner, A., Mizelle, J. D., and Conners, C. K. "A Psychopharmacologic Experiment in a Training School for Delinquent Boys: Methods, Problems, Findings." *American Journal of Orthopsychiatry,* 1963, *33,* 431–447.

Gittelman, R., Mannuzza, S., Shenker, R., and Bonagura, N. "Hyperactive Boys Almost Grown Up, I: Psychiatric Status." *Archives of General Psychiatry,* 1985, *42,* 937–947.

Goldberg, J. B., and Kurland, A. A. "Pimozide in the Treatment of Behavioral Disorders of Hospitalized Adolescents." *Journal of Clinical Pharmacology,* 1974, *14* (2), 134–139.

Lefkowitz, M. M. "Effects of Diphenylhydantoin on Disruptive Behavior: Study of Male Delinquents." *Archives of General Psychiatry*, 1969, *20*, 643–651.

Looker, A., and Conners, C. K. "Diphenylhydantoin in Children with Severe Temper Tantrums." *Archives of General Psychiatry*, 1970, *23*, 80–89.

Rifkin, A., Karajgi, B., Boppana, V., and Pearl, E. "Lithium Treatment in Hospitalized Adolescents with Conduct Disorder." Paper presented at the 29th annual meeting of the New Drug Clinical Evaluation Units, National Institute of Mental Health, Key Biscayne, Fla., May 1989.

Sheard, M. H., Marini, J. L., Bridges, C. I., and Wagner, E. "The Effect of Lithium on Impulsive Aggressive Behavior in Man." *American Journal of Psychiatry*, 1976, *133*, 1409–1413.

Tupin, J. P., Smith, D. B., Clanon, T. L., Kim, L. I., Nugent, A., and Groupe, A. "The Long-Term Use of Lithium in Aggressive Prisoners." *Comprehensive Psychiatry*, 1973, *14*, 311–317.

ARTHUR RIFKIN, *professor of psychiatry at the Albert Einstein College of Medicine and assistant director for academic affairs at the Hillside Hospital Division of the Long Island Jewish Medical Center (Jamaica, N.Y.), specializes in clinical psychopharmacological research.*

*Evidence from family, adoption and twin, and animal studies
indicates a strong hereditary-biological component to the
development of anxiety disorders; a substantial body of evidence
demonstrates important relationships between depression and
anxiety disorders, especially panic disorder.*

Anxiety Disorders

Bruce Black

Anxiety is a ubiquitous emotion, experienced to some degree by all
healthy people every day. Usually adaptive, anxiety increases alertness,
vigilance, and physiological responsiveness and enhances motivation.
Anxiety should only be regarded as symptomatic of a disorder when it is
excessive and maladaptive, causing psychosocial impairment or significant
distress for the person. Excessive maladaptive anxiety is the cardinal
symptom of a group of disorders classified as anxiety disorders. But
anxiety is also a common symptom of a number of other psychiatric disorders, including depression, psychotic disorders, and attention deficit
hyperactivity disorder.

Anxiety has cognitive, physiological, and behavioral components. The
most common cognitive symptoms are psychic distress, apprehension, and
dread. Heightened physiological arousal is marked by increased heart rate,
breathing, and muscular tension. Behavioral symptoms may include plead-
ing for help, fleeing, or avoiding anxiety-producing situations.

Many fears or anxieties in children are age specific: they are relatively
common at specific ages and are not generally a sign of an anxiety disorder.
For example, infants commonly go through periods of "stranger anxiety"
and "separation anxiety"; pre-school-age children often fear injury, masks,
and animals; teenagers may develop increased anxiety related to death, social
competence, and sexuality.

The DSM-III-R (American Psychiatric Association, 1987) classifies the
anxiety disorders as follows: overanxious disorder, separation anxiety disorder, avoidant disorder of childhood or adolescence, panic disorder with
or without agoraphobia, social phobia, simple phobia, obsessive-compulsive
disorder (see Chapter Three in this volume), posttraumatic stress disorder,

and generalized anxiety disorder. (The first three are applied only to children and adolescents.)

Overanxious disorder and *generalized anxiety disorder* are characterized by excessive or unrealistic anxiety or worry about various concerns. Somatic complaints such as headaches or stomach aches, perfectionist tendencies, and nervous habits are common. *Separation anxiety disorder* is characterized by excessive anxiety about separation from those to whom the child is attached. Common symptoms are unrealistic worries about possible harm befalling attachment figures, fear that they will not return home, worries of being lost or kidnapped, school refusal, reluctance to sleep alone, and complaints of physical symptoms associated with separations. The child's reaction to separation may be similar to panic attacks seen in patients with panic disorder.

Panic disorder and *separation anxiety disorder* may be closely related. Panic disorder is characterized by recurrent panic attacks: discrete periods of intense fear or discomfort accompanied by a variety of characteristic physical and emotional symptoms that occur unexpectedly and last for minutes to hours. Over time, many individuals afflicted with panic disorder develop a generalized anxiety called *anticipatory anxiety,* related to the fear of having an unpredictable panic attack. They may also develop specific phobias of places or circumstances associated with a prior attack. They may avoid settings—such as bridges and tunnels, crowded places, unfamiliar places, or even just being alone—in which they anticipate that it would be difficult to escape or get help. This phobic avoidant behavior is called *agoraphobia,* or *panic disorder with agoraphobia.*

Sufficiently severe to interfere with social functioning, *avoidant disorder of childhood or adolescence* is characterized by excessive shrinking from contact with unfamiliar people coupled with a clear desire for social involvement with familiar people, such as family and close friends. *Social phobia* is characterized by persistent fear of social situations in which the individual is exposed to possible scrutiny by others; the individual is afraid of doing something embarrassing or humiliating. Avoidant disorder may simply represent the childhood form of social phobia.

Characterized by a persistent fear of a circumscribed stimulus (for example, dogs, insects, snakes, rodents, thunderstorms) that almost invariably provokes an immediate anxiety response, *simple phobia* leads to avoidance of the stimulus. Only when such fears cause significant disability or suffering is the diagnosis of an anxiety disorder appropriate.

Posttraumatic stress disorder is characterized by the development of a number of characteristic symptoms following an extremely distressing traumatic event such as a severe accident, assault, or sexual abuse. The symptoms may include recurrent, intrusive thoughts about the traumatic event, numbing of emotional responsiveness, and increased arousal.

Children who refuse to go to school are sometimes referred to as suffering from "school phobia," but this is not an official diagnostic term. School refusal may be due to an anxiety disorder, most commonly separation anxiety disorder, or it may be due to another disorder—for example, depression or psychosis.

Not all individuals who suffer from an anxiety disorder fit neatly into one diagnostic category or another. Many individuals show symptoms of several diagnostic categories. For example, a child with separation anxiety and school refusal may also experience a great deal of anxiety in social situations and may have mild obsessions or compulsions. Further, anxiety disorders and depressive disorders are commonly associated at all ages.

Anxiety disorders are the most prevalent of all neurobiological disorders in adults, affecting approximately 15 percent of the adult population. Age fifteen is the average age at onset. Reliable data about the prevalence of anxiety disorders in children and adolescents are not available. We do know that specific fears are common in childhood, affecting 10 to 40 percent of school-age children, but many of these fears seem to cause little difficulty for the affected youngster and usually resolve over time without any specific treatment. Probably around 1 to 3 percent of children and adolescents suffer from a true anxiety disorder. Among school-age children, overanxious disorder and separation anxiety disorder are the most common anxiety disorders. The peak period of onset for panic disorder is in the mid teens.

Etiology and Neuropathophysiology

Evidence from family, adoption and twin, and animal studies as well as from studies of the developmental course of shy, temperamentally inhibited young children indicates a strong hereditary-biological component to the development of anxiety disorders. Studies of the young children of parents with panic disorder with agoraphobia have found that a high proportion show a behaviorally and physiologically characteristic pattern of response to novel situations called "behavioral inhibition to the unfamiliar." Behaviorally inhibited children are slower to speak, speak less, and have increased activity in the sympathetic nervous system in unfamiliar situations. This trait appears to show significant stability from infancy into childhood and adolescence. Twin studies have shown that the trait is inherited and that the degree of physiological reactivity to stress is also inherited and closely correlated to behavioral measures. Recent studies in humans and animals have examined the neurobiological mechanisms underlying these differences. Consistently inhibited children may have lower thresholds of excitability in the limbic system of the brain, particularly the amygdala and hypothalamus, leading to activation of the hypothalamic-pituitary-adrenal axis and sympathetic nervous system. Investigators have hypothesized that behavioral inhibition in young children may be a predictor of risk for the development of panic disorder.

Anxiety is an emotion we are all genetically programmed to experience. In fact, it may be "the first emotion" in terms of both an individual's emotional development and evolution. In evolution, the development of the brain structures that contain the programming for anxiety—the limbic system—and of behaviors that seem to be analogous with what we experience as anxiety appear in parallel with social attachment behaviors, especially mother-offspring attachment. Therefore, part of the adaptive role or evolutionary purpose of anxiety may be related to the enhancement of social attachment. Of course, anxiety also plays an adaptive role by helping us to avoid danger. This may be why we are genetically predisposed to phobias of some objects or situations over others—for example, animal, spider, and height phobias.

A substantial body of evidence has accumulated demonstrating important relationships between depression and anxiety disorders, especially panic disorder and separation anxiety disorder of childhood. Depression, panic disorder, and separation anxiety disorder of childhood commonly co-occur in the same individual. They also tend to aggregate within families, so that the family members of individuals with one of these disorders are also at increased risk for the other disorders. All three disorders respond to treatment with antidepressant medications. This relationship may reflect common pathophysiological abnormalities in the regulation of the affective response to the stress of separation experiences.

Animal separation distress has become a useful model for understanding the neurobiology and evolutionary history of anxiety. In rhesus monkeys, intra-individual differences in behavioral and physiological responses to social separations and other stress experiences are stable across the life span of individual animals. These individual "behavioral response styles" correlate with the response styles of genetic relatives and with the individual's vulnerability to develop maladaptive, anxiety-like or depression-like behaviors under stressful circumstances. The characteristic behavioral responses to maternal separation in young rhesus monkeys, isolation distress calls in squirrel monkeys, and distress vocalizations in puppies separated from litter mates are blocked by treatment with imipramine, a medication commonly used in the treatment of panic disorder. These animal studies have been crucial in scientific efforts to unravel the neuropharmacology and neuroanatomy of anxiety.

In humans, we know that adults with anxiety disorders, when compared to people without anxiety disorders, have a number of characteristic neurobiological abnormalities. The chemical neurotransmitter system in the brain known as the norepinephrine system appears to be abnormally regulated. These abnormalities may be associated with the *locus ceruleus*, the part of the brain that exerts primary control over the noradrenergic system. Abnormal distribution of brain blood flow and brain metabolic activity has also been demonstrated.

So-called challenge studies have contributed to our understanding of the biological basis and pathophysiology of anxiety and panic attacks. For example, when given intravenous infusions of sodium lactate solution, about 80 percent of patients with panic disorder develop panic attacks, compared to less than 10 percent of control subjects without anxiety disorders. Similar differences are found when a variety of medications that affect the norepinephrine and adenosine neurotransmitter systems in the brain are administered. To date, no studies have been done of the neuropathophysiology of anxiety disorders in children and adolescents.

Treatment and Progress

Behavioral and cognitive therapies, based on conditioning theory and empirical testing, appear to be effective for many children with anxiety disorders, especially simple phobia and separation disorder.

Psychotherapies other than behavioral therapies (particularly individual psychodynamic psychotherapy based on psychoanalytic theories) are very widely utilized in the treatment of anxiety disorders of childhood. When used alone, these forms of treatment are probably of little value, especially when rigidly applied based on guidelines derived from theory rather than based on empirical evidence. However, a close working relationship with a knowledgeable and skillful clinician can contribute to increased self-awareness and understanding in an anxious child or adolescent and in family members and is frequently a crucial element in successful treatment.

A variety of medications have been proven effective in treating anxiety disorders in adults. Although further study is very much needed, the same medications—the tricyclic antidepressants are the most commonly used—are generally effective in treating children and adolescents with anxiety disorders. The medications' precise mechanism of action in relieving anxiety symptoms is not known, but it is known that they cause alterations in the functioning of the same brain neurotransmitter systems that have been implicated in the pathophysiology of anxiety disorders.

We know little about what happens to anxious children as they grow up. Although these children are at increased risk of suffering from an anxiety disorder as adults compared to nonanxious children, most children with anxiety disorders do not appear to have anxiety disorders as adults.

Research Directions

We need to know much more about the phenomenology and long-term course of anxiety disorders in children and adolescents. Further epidemiological studies of clinical and nonclinical populations, plus prospective studies of children "at risk" for anxiety disorders, would increase our understanding of the early developmental course of these disorders and contribute greatly to our efforts to discern their etiology. Genetic linkage studies may yield further clues to the etiology of these disorders and their relationships to one another and to other brain disorders, such as depressive disorders. Long-term follow-up studies, also known as "outcome studies," will provide vital information for our assessment of various treatment interventions and will allow us to more knowledgeably advise people affected by anxiety disorders and their families regarding prognosis. There has been virtually no substantial research on the biology, pathophysiology, or pharmacological treatment of anxiety disorders in children and adolescents. Well-designed, systematic treatment studies are needed, and different forms of treatment need to be compared directly. Neuroendocrine function, neurotransmitter receptor activity, sleep and other chronobiological phenomena, and responses to clinical and experimental pharmacological agents need to be studied across the life span in humans with anxiety disorders and in animal models. These studies should further our understanding of the neuropathophysiology of anxiety disorders and the neurophysiology of the affective response to danger, loss, or separation.

Reference

American Psychiatric Association. *Diagnostic and Statistical Manual of Mental Disorders.* (DSM-III-R.) Washington, D.C.: American Psychiatric Association, 1987.

Additional Sources

Black, B., and Robbins, D. R. "Panic Disorder in Children and Adolescents." *Journal of the American Academy of Child and Adolescent Psychiatry,* 1990, *29* (1), 36–44.

Gittelman, R. (ed.). *Anxiety Disorders of Childhood.* New York: Guilford Press, 1986.

Kagan, J., and Reznick, S. "Biological Bases of Childhood Shyness." *Science,* 1988, *240,* 167–172.

Klein, R. G., and Last, C. G. *Anxiety Disorders in Children.* Newbury Park, Calif.: Sage, 1989.

McDermott, J. F., Werry, J., Petti, T., Combrinck-Graham, L., and Char, W. F. "Anxiety Disorders of Childhood or Adolescence." In *Treatments of Psychiatric Disorders: A Task Force Report of the American Psychiatric Association.* Vol. 1. Washington, D.C.: American Psychiatric Association, 1989.

BRUCE BLACK is senior staff fellow and director of the Anxiety Disorders Outpatient Program, Section on Anxiety and Affective Disorders, in the Biological Psychiatry Branch of the National Institute of Mental Health.

Schizophrenia has been described in children as young as five years of age and should be a diagnostic consideration in any child with psychosis.

Childhood-Onset Schizophrenia

Charles T. Gordon

Schizophrenia, a severe, chronic psychotic illness affecting about 1 percent of the population, is equally common in males and females worldwide. Psychotic symptoms required for the diagnosis include delusions, hallucinations, disorganized thought processes, bizarre behavior, and flat or grossly inappropriate affect. Delusions are false, often fragmented, bizarre beliefs. Patients often have numerous delusions whose content may vary. Commonly observed kinds of delusions are paranoid (belief that others are spying on, or trying to harm, the person), grandiose (belief that the person has special powers or abilities), somatic (belief that one's body is diseased, abnormal, or changed), thought broadcasting (belief that one's thoughts are being broadcast to the outside world), thought insertion or withdrawal (belief that thoughts that are not one's own are inserted into, or removed from, one's mind), and delusions of being controlled (belief that one's thoughts or actions are imposed by an external force). Hallucinations are usually auditory, visual, or tactile but may also involve olfactory or gustatory phenomena. Disorganized thought process is manifest by loose associations: ideas shift from one subject to an unrelated, or obliquely related, subject without the person's demonstrating awareness that the subjects are unconnected. Bizarre behavior may include unusual postures and mannerisms. Flat affect is a marked diminution in the verbal and nonverbal expression of emotion (monotonous voice, immobile face). Inappropriate affect means the emotional expression is incongruent with the content of the person's ideation (for example, laughing while talking about being pursued by an enemy). Marked social withdrawal, impairment in hygiene, and decrease in initiative, interests, and energy are commonly associated with these psychotic symptoms. An illness duration of at least six months and a

NEW DIRECTIONS FOR MENTAL HEALTH SERVICES, no. 54, Summer 1992 © Jossey-Bass Publishers

decline in social and occupational functioning are required for the diagnosis.

Variability in age at onset has been noted since Emil Kraepelin first described schizophrenia nearly 100 years ago. Commonly, onset of psychotic symptoms and diagnosis of schizophrenia occur in the early to mid twenties, but onset of psychosis has been described as early as age five and as late as age seventy. Childhood-onset schizophrenia is defined here as onset of psychosis prior to the twelfth birthday. There is little information on the incidence and prevalence of schizophrenia with onset in childhood, but it is assumed to be rare. In terms of symptomatology and other diagnostic features, children are similar to adults and the same diagnostic criteria are used whatever the age at onset. Uncertainties exist about the relationship of childhood-onset schizophrenia to autism-spectrum disorders and adult-onset schizophrenia. It is likely that there are at least two groups within the childhood-onset schizophrenia group; one related to autism and the other to adult schizophrenia.

Symptoms characteristic of schizophrenia occur in other childhood neurobiological disorders, so that these must be carefully ruled out when evaluating a child with psychosis. Childhood major depression can be accompanied by hallucinations and delusions and may be very difficult to differentiate from schizophrenia because depressive symptomatology may be part of the early course of schizophrenic illness. Mania, pervasive developmental disorders (PDD), obsessive-compulsive disorder, multiple personality disorder, expressive language disorder, and a host of developmental, postinfectious, and metabolic organic mental disorders can mimic schizophrenia.

Etiology, Neuroanatomy, and Pathophysiology

It is generally accepted that schizophrenia is a heterogeneous disorder (with multiple underlying causes resulting in a common clinical presentation) and that both genetic and nongenetic factors play a role in its etiology. Family, adoption, and twin studies all provide evidence for a genetic component. For example, first-degree relatives of patients with schizophrenia have a 10 percent risk of schizophrenia, whereas the general population's risk is 1 percent. The concordance rate in monozygotic (identical) twins is approximately 50 percent; it is about 10 percent in dizygotic (fraternal) twins. The precise nature of nongenetic influences is unknown, but theories include infectious, anoxic, autoimmune, and metabolic insults during prenatal or childhood development. There is no evidence that childhood-onset illness differs etiologically from illness with later onset. Childhood onset could result from a "heavier" genetic load or a more potent nongenetic insult. Neurobiological findings in the childhood-onset group will be less obscured by chronic institutionalization, long-term neuroleptic treatment, and substance abuse. Hence, systematic study of brain structure and function in the earliest-onset cases may provide an as yet unexplored avenue in clinical schizophrenia research.

Computerized axial tomography (CAT) scan and magnetic resonance imaging (MRI) in adults with schizophrenia have consistently shown slightly enlarged cerebral ventricles (the fluid-filled brain compartments), reduced volume of medial temporal lobe structures, and abnormalities of the corpus callosum. Functional brain imaging studies, including positron emission tomography (PET) and single photon emission computerized tomography (SPECT) scans, have revealed diminished activity of the prefrontal cortex in adults with schizophrenia. Neurochemical studies, extensively carried out in adults with schizophrenia, have yielded many contradictory findings, perhaps due to sample heterogeneity and failure to control for level of motor activity, age, sex, height, dietary habits, drug treatment, and seasonal variation. The most enduring biochemical etiological hypothesis of adult schizophrenia is the dopamine hypothesis that proposes that enhanced dopaminergic transmission is causally related to the disease. This hypothesis is primarily based on the antipsychotic effects of dopamine-blocking drugs and the psychosis-producing effects of dopamine enhancers (such as amphetamines). Serotonin abnormalities may also play an important role. To date, due to small sample sizes and nonstandardized diagnostic criteria, no conclusions can be drawn from the few neurochemical studies done in childhood-onset schizophrenia.

In the Child Psychiatry Branch at the National Institute of Mental Health (NIMH), we are now performing the first brain imaging studies (MRI and PET) in childhood-onset schizophrenia. We hypothesize that a subgroup of childhood-onset cases will have imaging findings similar to adults with schizophrenia, and another subgroup will exhibit more generalized, nonspecific findings (phenocopies). We are also doing extensive biochemical studies in childhood-onset cases. We hypothesize two subgroups: one with increased dopaminergic function and the other with primarily serotonergic dysfunction.

Medical Management of Childhood-Onset Schizophrenia

Just as the etiology of schizophrenia is unknown, so is the definitive cure. The usual course over many years is one of acute exacerbations of psychosis with residual impairment between episodes. In adults with schizophrenia, antipsychotic medications have proven quite useful in decreasing psychotic symptoms and improving social and occupational functioning, especially when used as part of a multimodal treatment plan that may include family education and support, social skills training, individual and group supportive/behavioral interventions, vocational rehabilitation, and supervised housing.

Approximately 20 percent of adult patients with schizophrenia respond poorly to typical antipsychotic medications. Another group is unable to tolerate the neurological side effects, including tardive dyskinesia (TD), a chronic involuntary movement disorder that most often involves the tongue and facial muscles as well as the extremities. For these two groups of patients, the atypical antipsychotic medication clozapine (Clozaril) has been helpful. This is because of its antipsychotic efficacy in people who do not respond to typical antipsychotic medications and because of the much reduced frequency of neurological side effects, including TD. But clozapine has two disadvantages: it is expensive, and a patient requires weekly blood monitoring because a possible complication of treatment is a dangerous lowering of the white blood count.

Little is known about the response of childhood-onset schizophrenia to psychotropic medications. At the NIMH, we are currently carrying out a study comparing the typical antipsychotic haloperidol (Haldol) with the atypical antipsychotic clozapine. We hypothesize that a large number of childhood-onset cases will be resistant to haloperidol and respond well to clozapine.

For parents of a child with psychosis, the first step is to have the child undergo a detailed diagnostic evaluation, because treatment recommendations follow from diagnosis. Often the most accurate diagnosis is not schizophrenia but another neurobiological disorder (such as PDD, major depression, and so on), which may require a very different treatment. The best place to begin the diagnostic process is usually with a child psychiatrist experienced at working with severely ill children, including those with psychosis, autism, obsessive-compulsive disorder, and multiple personality disorder—all of which are often confused with schizophrenia. Depending on the child's level of functioning, the evaluation may be done on an inpatient or outpatient basis. The child psychiatrist, who should coordinate the diagnostic evaluation, may wish to get consultations from a pediatric neurologist (to rule out reversible neurological disorders), a psychologist (to define cognitive deficits through neuropsychological testing), and a speech pathologist (to rule out expressive language disorder, which may be confused with thought disorder).

Once a working diagnosis of childhood-onset schizophrenia is made, the child psychiatrist should coordinate a multidisciplinary treatment approach consisting of antipsychotic medication, family education and support, educational intervention (special education is usually required), and sometimes social skills training and behavior therapy. Throughout the treatment process, the issue of correct diagnosis should be continuously evaluated.

Research Directions

Systematic investigation of childhood-onset schizophrenia is still in its infancy because the rarity of the disorder and diagnostic confusion have seriously impeded informative research. Useful clinical descriptions of presenting psychotic and associated symptomatology, developmental course, and neuropsychological profile have emerged over the past five years. Now the NIMH is doing studies of genetics, neurobiology (imaging and biochemistry), and pharmacological response. These studies will hopefully shed light on the relationship of childhood-onset schizophrenia to other childhood psychotic disorders and later-onset schizophrenia. They will also form the basis for more rational and systematic diagnosis and treatment of children with psychosis.

Additional Sources

Beitchman, J. H. "Childhood Schizophrenia: A Review and Comparison with Adult Onset Schizophrenia." *Psychiatric Clinics of North America,* 1985, *8,* 793–814.

Green, W., Campbell, M., Hardesty, A., Grega, D., Padron-Gayol, M., Shell, J., and Erlenmeyer-Kimling, L. "A Comparison of Schizophrenic and Autistic Children." *Journal of the American Academy of Child and Adolescent Psychiatry,* 1984, *23,* 399–409.

Russell, A., Bott, L., and Sammons, C. "The Phenomenology of Schizophrenia Occurring in Childhood." *Journal of the American Academy of Child and Adolescent Psychiatry,* 1989, *28,* 399–407.

Watkins, J., Asarnow, R., and Tanguay, P. "Symptom Development in Childhood Onset Schizophrenia." *Journal of Child Psychology and Psychiatry,* 1988, *29,* 865–878.

CHARLES T. GORDON, senior staff fellow in the Child Psychiatry Branch, National Institute of Mental Health, is currently carrying out some of the first studies of the neurobiology and pharmacology of childhood-onset schizophrenia.

Neuroimaging techniques are beginning to unlock the mysteries of how the structure and function of the brain are abnormal in patients with mental illness.

Neuroimaging in Neuropsychiatry

Daniel R. Weinberger

Of all the dramatic advances in the neurosciences, none has had a greater impact on the study of patients with disorders of the brain than neuroimaging techniques. Prior to the development of the computerized axial tomography (CAT) scan in the early 1970s, it was almost impossible to identify before death the exact location and cause of a change in the brain's function. But with the advent of modern neuroimaging, it has become possible to visualize in great detail the structure and the function of the living brain and to identify specific sites and causes of abnormalities. These new imaging techniques are now the principal tools for diagnosing a wide variety of neurological disorders such as brain tumors, stroke, Alzheimer's disease, and multiple sclerosis. Modern neuroimaging has also made it possible to test a number of hypotheses concerning the role of abnormalities in both structure and function at specific sites in the brain in a number of neurobiological disorders (such as obsessive-compulsive disorder, schizophrenia, and so on).

CAT and MRI Scans

The CAT scanner is a radiological device that uses low-energy radiation (x-rays), advanced electronics, and sophisticated computer mathematics to produce detailed, accurate images of the inside of the brain. The images, displayed as cross-sectional "slices" analogous to the slices in a loaf of bread, reflect subtle variations in the density of structures within the brain.

The magnetic resonance imaging (MRI) scanner differs fundamentally from the CAT scanner because it does not use any x-rays for image production. Instead, the MRI scanner uses a very strong magnetic field, radio waves,

NEW DIRECTIONS FOR MENTAL HEALTH SERVICES, no. 54, Summer 1992 © Jossey-Bass Publishers

and sophisticated computer technology to produce anatomical images or "slices" (similar to the CAT scan slices) that reflect subtle variations in the magnetic properties of atoms within different parts of the brain.

Many brain diseases result in abnormalities in either (1) the density of the tissues in specific brain regions, which can be detected on a CAT scan, or (2) the magnetic properties of brain tissues, which can be detected on an MRI scan. As a result, such diseases can often be diagnosed by recognizable, reproducible aberrations in the appearance of either a CAT or an MRI scan. A major advantage of CAT and MRI scans is that neither procedure is invasive and both are completely painless.

In clinical practice today, the MRI scan is often the procedure of choice because it involves no exposure to ionizing radiation; thus, for the overwhelming majority of patients, the MRI scan has no known risks or hazards. Also, the MRI scan, which produces more detailed images than the CAT scan, can often demonstrate abnormalities in the brain that the CAT scan may miss. Because the MRI scan does not use ionizing radiation, it is especially valuable for examining infants and children. The only current disadvantages of the MRI scan compared to the CAT scan are increased cost; the sometimes intense experience of confinement for the patient during an MRI scan, which makes it a difficult procedure for claustrophobic patients; and problems posed by some patients with internal metal objects (such as cardiac pacemakers or surgical clips), who may not be suitable candidates for an MRI scan because of the very intense magnetic field used in the scanning process.

PET and SPECT Scans

Positron emission tomography (PET) and single photon emission computerized tomography (SPECT) are nuclear medicine techniques that involve very small amounts of radioactivity. With both methods, a radioactive chemical compound is introduced into the bloodstream, usually by intravenous infusion, and the compound is then concentrated within the brain. The PET or SPECT scanner, which surrounds the patient's head, detects the emission of gamma rays from the radioactive compound concentrated in the brain. With computerized techniques similar to those used in CAT scanning, it is possible to produce images (brain "slices" similar to CAT scanning) that represent the distribution of the radioactive compound within the brain. A variety of physiological and chemical processes can be studied with these techniques. For example, glucose metabolism, a fundamental measure of brain function, can be studied with PET by injecting radioactive glucose into the patient and then measuring the relative concentration of this radioactive glucose within the brain. Regional cerebral blood flow, another sensitive measure of brain activity closely linked to glucose metabolism, can be studied with either PET or SPECT using various radioactive compounds that are a "tracer" of blood flow. The specific concentrations of other chemicals (such as dopamine, serotonin, acetylcholine, and so on) at diverse sites within the brain can be imaged in a similar way.

In general, both PET and SPECT techniques are expensive, time consuming, involve some discomfort, and expose the patient to small amounts of radiation. At present, both techniques are primary research tools that have no accepted role in the routine evaluation of patients with neurobiological disorders. Because both methods involve some radiation exposure, they have been used very little in research studies of either infants or children. But in adults, where the limits of radiation exposure are less stringent, extensive research has been conducted with both PET and SPECT.

CAT and MRI Scanning in Psychiatric Disorders

Even though most MRI and CAT scans of psychiatric patients tend to be interpreted as grossly "normal," the past decade of research has demonstrated that certain psychiatric disorders are *consistently and reproducibly* associated with quantitative anatomical deviations. For example, over 100 CAT and MRI studies worldwide have demonstrated that patients with schizophrenia tend to have slightly enlarged cerebral ventricles and more prominent cortical sulci than normal individuals of the same age (Zigun and Weinberger, 1992). These findings have led to speculation that schizophrenia may be caused by a subtle change in brain anatomy that results in a slight reduction in brain volume. *The fact that these studies have demonstrated conclusively that anatomical-biological changes in the brain, which can be measured by CAT or MRI scans, are associated with schizophrenia is revolutionary.* It must be emphasized that the ventricular and cortical sulci enlargement in patients with schizophrenia is subtle; therefore, it is impossible to use CAT or MRI scanning alone to diagnose schizophrenia or even to determine the extent to which a particular patient with schizophrenia has altered brain anatomy. But in spite of the limitations of CAT and MRI neuroimaging, the research evidence suggests that subtle anatomical changes characterize most patients with schizophrenia. Recent studies of identical twins, where one twin has schizophrenia and the other twin does not, have revealed that the cerebral ventricles were slightly larger in the twin with schizophrenia in almost every case (Suddath and others, 1990).

In addition, because MRI provides scans of such extraordinary anatomical detail, it has been possible to identify discrete areas of the brain where a reduction in brain volume has taken place. The studies in twin and in nontwin populations have revealed a tendency for the brain volume reduction to include the hippocampus, a region of the brain associated with the limbic system. Again, it must be emphasized that these volume differences are very slight, and unless an unaffected twin is available for study, such subtle changes may not be appreciated in every affected individual.

Several studies of adolescent patients with schizophrenia have confirmed that the subtle anatomical changes described above also exist in young patients. More important, these anatomical changes exist at the onset of the illness (Weinberger and others, 1982; Bogerts and others, 1990). For the most part, studies that have followed patients for several years after the onset of the illness have revealed that the CAT and MRI findings do not change over time. These observations have supported speculation that the brain changes in schizophrenia represent fixed structural defects or "vulnerability," perhaps the result of a process affecting brain development during gestation, and are not the result of an injury or insult that begins in adolescence or early adult life (Weinberger, 1987).

A number of other neurobiological disorders have been the subject of CAT and MRI scanning studies. Some adult patients with mood disorders have enlarged ventricles, but this finding has not been reported in adolescent subjects at the onset of the illness. Enlarged ventricles have been reported in patients with pervasive developmental disorders and autism, but other studies have failed to confirm these observations (Feinstein and Weinberger, 1987). A recent report of a consistent reduction in the size of the cerebellum in autistic patients has created a great deal of excitement (Courchesne and others, 1988; see Chapter Two in this volume). Other reports, however, have questioned the universality of this finding in autistic patients. MRI and CAT studies of patients with a variety of other diagnoses, including attention deficit disorder, Tourette's syndrome, and obsessive-compulsive disorder, have found no consistent subtle abnormalities in brain anatomy.

PET and SPECT Studies in Psychiatric Disorders

PET and SPECT studies of patients with psychiatric disorders have been more difficult to interpret than the CAT and MRI studies. In studies where PET or SPECT suggest brain function abnormalities associated with psychiatric disorders, these abnormalities have been of a quantitative rather than of a qualitative nature. Also, because most brain functions such as glucose metabolism or cerebral blood flow vary greatly from one individual to another, the findings of the PET and SPECT studies reflect tendencies in large groups of patients and not characteristics of individual subjects.

The most significant finding from the imaging studies on brain function has been a trend in patients with schizophrenia to have reduced function of the frontal lobes (Weinberger and Berman, 1988). This finding has also been described in adolescent patients at the onset of the illness. In the study of twins, where normal variability is minimized, *reduced frontal lobe function has been found in the affected twin in every twin pair studied.*

This suggests that a relative decrease in frontal lobe function may be characteristic of schizophrenia. Less frequently replicated findings, such as reduced brain function in depression and increased temporal lobe function in anxiety, have also been reported. Studies of brain function in childhood neurobiological disorders such as autism and attention deficit disorder have been rare and have not produced well-replicated results.

Role of Neuroimaging in Evaluating Patients with a Neurobiological Disorder

While the results noted above indicate that neuroimaging techniques cannot be used to make the diagnosis of a neurobiological disorder or to help in the application of therapy, they are, nonetheless, important in the clinical evaluation of patients with psychiatric disorders. Since many neurological diseases (for example, brain tumors) can masquerade as a psychiatric condition, it is essential to rule out this possibility in evaluating every patient. This can be accomplished easily and harmlessly with an MRI scan. Guidelines for when to order an MRI scan in an adult patient have been published (Weinberger, 1990). Because the MRI scan involves no ionizing radiation, it is particularly appropriate for children and adolescents. With the exception of CAT scanning, other non-MRI neuroimaging techniques have no current role in routine clinical practice. CAT scanning may be a useful substitute for MRI when (1) MRI scanning is unavailable, (2) MRI scanning cannot be tolerated due to claustrophobia, or (3) MRI scanning is contraindicated due to internal metal devices in the patient.

Future Neuroimaging Studies

The capacity to measure neurochemical activity in the living brain has great potential for future research. A number of hypotheses about the etiology of psychiatric illnesses that have stressed chemical abnormalities may be testable with PET and SPECT methods. For example, the "dopamine hypothesis" of schizophrenia has been tested in several preliminary studies using PET and a radioactive compound that binds to dopamine receptors in the brain. While the results of these studies have not been conclusive, the feasibility of such studies has been established. Eventually, these techniques may be useful in selecting proper drug therapy, including the choice and dose of medication.

References

Bogerts, B., Ashtari, M., Degreef, G., Alvir, J., Bilder, R. M., and Lieberman, J. A. "Reduced Temporal Limbic Structure Volumes on Magnetic Resonance Images in First Episode Schizophrenia." *Psychiatry Research: Neuroimaging*, 1990, 35, 1–13.

Courchesne, E., Yeung-Courchesne, R., Press, G. A., Hesselink, J. R., and Jernigan, T. "Hypo-
  plasia of Cerebellar Vermal Lobules VI and VII in Autism." *New England Journal of Medicine,*
  1988, *318,* 1349–1354.
Feinstein, C., and Weinberger, D. R. "Brain Imaging: Relevance to Child Psychiatry." In J.
  Noshpitz (ed.), *Handbook of Child Psychiatry,* Vol. 5. New York: Basic Books, 1987.
Suddath, R. L., Christison, G. W., Torrey, E. F., Casanova, M. F., and Weinberger, D. R. "Ana-
  tomical Abnormalities in the Brains of Monozygotic Twins Discordant for Schizophrenia."
  New England Journal of Medicine, 1990, *322,* 789–794.
Weinberger, D. R. "Implications of Normal Brain Development for the Pathogenesis of Schiz-
  ophrenia." *Archives of General Psychiatry,* 1987, *44,* 660–669.
Weinberger, D. R. "Structural and Functional Brain Imaging in Psychiatry." *Journal of Clinical
  Brain Imaging,* 1990, *1,* 3–9.
Weinberger, D. R., and Berman, K. F. "Speculation on the Meaning of Cerebral Metabolic
  'Hypofrontality' in Schizophrenia." *Schizophrenia Bulletin,* 1988, *14,* 179–184.
Weinberger, D. R., DeLisi, L. E., Perman, G., Targum, S., and Wyatt, R. J. "Computed Tomog-
  raphy Scans in Schizophreniform Disorder and Other Acute Psychiatric Patients." *Archives
  of General Psychiatry,* 1982, *39,* 778–783.
Zigun, J., and Weinberger, D. R. "In Vivo Studies of Brain Morphology in Patients with
  Schizophrenia." In J.-P. Lindenmayer and S. R. Kay (eds.), *New Biological Vistas on Schizo-
  phrenia.* New York: Bruner/Mazel, 1992.

DANIEL R. WEINBERGER *is chief of the Clinical Brain Disorders Branch of the
Intramural Research Program at the National Institute of Mental Health Neuroscience Center at St. Elizabeth's, Washington, D.C.*

New technologies in the neurosciences offer major opportunities to better understand and treat the severe neurobehavioral and neurobiological disorders of childhood and adolescence.

Future Directions in Neuroscience Research for Twentieth-Century Child and Adolescent Psychiatry

Peter S. Jensen

During the last decade, significant advances have been made in unraveling some of the mysteries of the brain and determining their relationship to severe neurobehavioral disorders. Simultaneously, significant strides have been made in establishing the relevance of these findings to children and adolescents (National Institute of Mental Health, 1990). While we are learning about the impact of these disorders on our children and youth, technological breakthroughs and research findings are also providing new opportunities to develop effective treatments for the major neurobehavioral and neurobiological disorders in child and adolescent populations.

Moreover, scientific advances are being realized in many areas. For example, new treatments affecting the serotonin neurotransmitter system have yielded dramatic improvement in obsessive-compulsive disorder (OCD) (Leonard and others, 1988). Genetic factors have been implicated in schizophrenia, bipolar disorder, Tourette's syndrome, OCD, autism, and certain learning disabilities like dyslexia (Ciaranello and Ciaranello, 1991; Leckman and Pauls, 1990). Brain imaging techniques now enable researchers to examine the brain's architecture, electrical activity, and metabolism in children and adolescents.

Though heartening, this progress is not sufficient. Current estimates are that over 7.5 million children and adolescents suffer from significant mental disorders (National Institute of Mental Health, 1990). It is widely accepted that, to varying degrees, all these disorders have major biological components in their etiology, onset, and maintenance of symptoms. Because of the devastating nature of these disorders of childhood and adolescence and the relatively slow rate of progress in understanding and treating them, the NIMH has developed the *National Plan for Research on Child and Adolescent Mental Disorders* (National Institute of Mental Health, 1990), a major program designed to greatly expand research activities on child and adolescent disorders. Under the *National Plan,* major new research initiatives are being formulated to increase our understanding of the causes and determinants of child and adolescent psychopathology; determine the effectiveness of biological, psychotherapeutic, and social treatments; develop more effective service delivery systems; and enlarge our cadre of qualified, committed researchers.

Implications of Basic Science Research for Clinical Disorders

The basic sciences—in particular the developmental neurosciences—offer great promise for major advances in the next decade, as foreseen by the NIMH's *National Plan.* The lines of investigation and technologies that seem most likely to result in significant new findings and define future research directions are discussed below.

A better understanding of the brain mechanisms that underlie the development and control of abnormal behavior is a central, critical research direction for the NIMH in the foreseeable future. What structural and functional changes of the brain's neural circuits occur across the life span? How do early abnormalities in the unfolding of this process relate to the neurobehavioral disorders of children and adolescents? Answering such questions will require careful development of several lines of investigation, such as these: (1) Which central nervous system processes are affected by poor prenatal care, prematurity, low birth weight, and childbirth complications, with the result that the person is likely to develop a neurobiological disorder? (2) What are the effects of biological "insults," like physical brain trauma or exposure to toxic chemicals or drugs? (3) What is the role of cognitive impairments (like those resulting from mental retardation, brain damage, learning disabilities) and deficits in sensory perception (including deafness and blindness) in the development of severe neurobehavioral disorders? (4) What is the impact of the brain's hormonal environment on the development and activity of the brain's neural circuits? At what points in development are these effects most pronounced? (5) What is the role of genetic factors in normal and abnormal social, emotional, and cognitive development? To a significant extent, the new technologies available to research scientists—including brain imaging techniques, genetic studies, biological markers of clinical disorders, and animal models—will make it possible to answer these questions.

Brain Imaging Techniques. Using CAT, MRI, and PET techniques, scientists have found abnormalities in the cerebral cortex and cerebellum in samples of patients with neurobiological disorders (Kuperman and others, 1990; see Chapters Two and Twelve in this volume). With the aid of PET scans, scientists have demonstrated abnormalities in glucose metabolism in certain areas of the brain in patients with OCD and in adults with attention deficit hyperactivity disorder (ADHD) (Benkelfat and others, 1990; Zametkin and others, 1990; see Chapters Three and Seven in this volume). Interestingly, treatment with specific pharmacological agents (for example, clomipramine in OCD and stimulants in ADHD) tends to normalize the metabolic activity levels in some of these patients, who also show concurrent clinical improvements (Benkelfat and others, 1990; Zametkin and others, 1990).

Imaging studies like the above should be repeated to confirm these preliminary findings, and they should also be carried out for differing kinds of brain activation (for example, during various learning tasks or states of emotional arousal). While there are ethical barriers to doing PET studies with children because of radiation exposure, alternative technologies for studying brain electrical activity are becoming available (for instance, brain electrical activity mapping) and should be used to pursue such studies in children (Kuperman and others, 1990).

Genetic Studies. Rapid advances in genetics research and the genetic study of neurobiological disorders have opened new doors to understanding how these disorders arise in children and adolescents. As it is becoming possible to map the human genome, it also will be possible to identify virtually any gene or group of genes that causes disorders presumed to be hereditary. Genetically informative research designs should be given high priority in basic, clinical, and epidemiological studies. Necessary studies include investigation of how the genes are controlled and how these control mechanisms regulate the early development of the nervous system. Such investigations may yield great breakthroughs in understanding the development of disorders such as autism, childhood-onset schizophrenia, and mood disorders (Leckman and Pauls, 1990).

There is a great need for genetic linkage studies of childhood-onset neurobiological disorders that have behavioral symptoms, like autism, anxiety disorders, ADHD, and Tourette's syndrome. Such studies are likely to indicate the location of genes related to the development of these severe conditions. In addition, proposed and ongoing genetic linkage studies of neurobiological disorders in adults, such as mood disorders or schizophrenia, whose onset can be in childhood or adolescence, should include children and adolescents in the study populations.

Biological Markers of Clinical Disorders. There has been some success in identifying biological correlates associated with certain patterns of behavior and specific traits correlated with certain clinical disorders. Thus, it has been fairly well documented that there is an inverse relationship between certain neurotransmitters and their metabolites in the cerebral spinal fluid and aggressive-impulsivity in adults (particularly males); recently, such findings have been extended to children and adolescents (Kruesi and others, 1990). Clearly, as technologies evolve, an increased focus in this area of research will emerge. Coupling the presence of neurochemical markers with genetic linkage studies, a better understanding of genetic factors in a number of the severe disorders should be possible and may serve to identify treatment-responsive subgroups.

Animal Models. Many advances in the understanding of biological contributions to psychopathology and related changes in the central nervous system (CNS) have come from the study of animals. For example, animal models have allowed the examination of factors such as lead-induced CNS lesions in ADHD. Animal studies to advance the understanding of basic biological contributions to development and to psychopathology in children and adolescents are critical for the growth of the developmental neurosciences and must be continued.

Conclusion

Technologies are developing rapidly, but the number of science researchers with the necessary skills to embark on basic biological investigations is in critically short supply. The Institute of Medicine (1989) study reported that fewer than twenty full-time academic child psychiatrists devote 80 percent or more of their time to scientific research of these disorders. Research careers in child and adolescent neuroscience need to be supported through further federal funding. The scope of research envisioned in the *National Plan for Research on Child and Adolescent Mental Disorders* is far reaching, and the range of critical research questions is enormous. A vigorous research agenda coupled with an extensive public and private commitment of time and resources should reap great benefits not only for all children and adolescents who suffer from severe neurobehavioral and neurobiological disorders, but also for families, friends, and society. Although the scientific study of these severe disorders in children has had a slow, difficult start, the time is right for the field's rapid expansion and our full dedication. Let us begin now.

References

Benkelfat, C., Nordahl, T. E., Semple, W. E., King, C., Murphy, D. L., and Cohen, R. M. "Local Cerebral Glucose Metabolic Rates in Obsessive-Compulsive Disorder." *Archives of General Psychiatry,* 1990, *47,* 840–848.

Ciaranello, R. D., and Ciaranello, A. L. "Genetics of Major Psychiatric Disorders." *Annual Review of Medicine,* 1991, *42,* 151–158.

Institute of Medicine. *Research on Children and Adolescents with Mental, Behavioral, and Developmental Disorders.* Publication no. IOM-89-07. Washington, D.C.: National Academy Press, 1989.

Kruesi, M.J.P., Rapoport, J. L., Hamburger, S., Hibbs, E., Potter, W. Z., Lenane, M., and Brown, G. L. "Cerebrospinal Fluid Monoamine Metabolites, Aggression, and Impulsivity in Disruptive Behavior Disorders of Children and Adolescents." *Archives of General Psychiatry,* 1990, *47,* 419–426.

Kuperman, S., Gaffney, G. R., Hamdan-Allen, G., Preston, D. F., and Venkatesh, L. "Neuroimaging in Child and Adolescent Psychiatry." *Journal of the American Academy of Child and Adolescent Psychiatry,* 1990, *29,* 159–172.

Leckman, J. F., and Pauls, D. L. "Genetics and Child Psychiatry." *Journal of the American Academy of Child and Adolescent Psychiatry,* 1990, *29,* 174–176.

Leonard, H., Swedo, S., Rapoport, J. L., Coffey, M., and Cheslow, D. "Treatment of Childhood Obsessive-Compulsive Disorder with Clomipramine and Desmethylimipramine: A Double-Blind Cross-Over Comparison." *Psychopharmacology Bulletin,* 1988, *24,* 93–95.

National Institute of Mental Health. *National Plan for Research on Child and Adolescent Mental Disorders: A Report Requested by the U.S. Congress.* Department of Health and Human Services publication no. (ADM) 90-1683. Washington, D.C.: U.S. Government Printing Office, 1990.

Zametkin, A. J., Nordahl, T. E., Gross, M., King, A. C., Semple, W. E., Rumsey, J., Hamburger, S., and Cohen, R. M. "Cerebral Glucose Metabolism in Adults with Hyperactivity of Childhood Onset." *New England Journal of Medicine,* 1990, *323,* 1361–1366.

PETER S. JENSEN is chief, Child and Adolescent Disorders Research Branch, and chair, Child and Adolescent Mental Disorders Research Consortium, National Institute of Mental Health.

PART TWO:

Future Directions for Society Based on the Neurobiological Revolution

It is time for our society's institutions to translate the scientific findings about neurobiological disorders into effective, reality-based actions.

Integrating the Neurobiological Revolution into Child and Adolescent Psychiatry and into Society

Richard Peschel, Enid Peschel

A revolution is underway in molecular biology and neurobiology. As Part One of this volume demonstrates, this scientific revolution is dramatically changing our fundamental understanding of many "psychiatric" disorders in children and adolescents. Neurobiological research has documented that many disorders in children and youth—including autism and pervasive developmental disorders, bipolar and major depressive disorders, obsessive-compulsive disorder, Tourette's syndrome, attention deficit hyperactivity disorder, schizophrenia, and anxiety disorders—are characterized by demonstrable malfunctions or malformations of the brain, or both.

Unfortunately, most of the institutions that interact with children and youth—including the health care industry, educational programs, legislative and governmental bodies, and the legal system—have not yet accepted the new scientific findings about the biological basis of many of these disorders, which are still categorized as "psychiatric" or "mental health" problems. This reflects the fact that so many of the medical, educational, social, governmental, and legal programs that currently deliver services and treatments to children and youth developed out of the nineteenth- and early-twentieth-century tradition that viewed these serious brain disorders as "mental" or "psychological" illness. Thus, most programs now in place largely ignore, or refuse to accept, the findings of the neuroscientific revolution of the last ten years. Indeed, our society as a whole tends to perceive and react to children with severe "psychiatric" disorders *without the benefit of, and knowledge about, the most recent scientific informa-tion.* Until we can integrate the newest neurobiological findings into the fabric and consciousness of society as a whole, the revolution in neurobiol-ogy will remain only a collection of scientific facts, divorced from their logical implications in terms of medical, educational, and social actions. It is time for the institutions of our society to translate these revolutionary scientific findings into effective, reality-based actions.

Need for Appropriate Scientific Language and Classification

The development of suitable language and classification must follow scien-tific discovery.

Language. The revolution in neuroscientific knowledge requires a cor-responding revolution in language. It is time to discard the inaccurate terms of the past that called brain disorders "mental" illness or "emotional" or "behavioral" disorders. These terms ignore the underlying scientific and biological basis of these brain disorders.

To assimilate the neuroscientific data into medical and everyday lan-guage, the specific disorders discussed in this book have been renamed *neu-robiological disorders (NBD)*. Another appropriate name would be *biologically based brain diseases (BBBD)*. These terms not only reflect the recent findings of the neuroscience revolution; they also help destigmatize these devastating physical disorders and the human beings who suffer from them.

Classification. Most of the major institutions that must care for, and deal with, children and adolescents with psychiatric problems have not properly defined their programs and policies according to a classification system that recognizes the research findings in neurobiology. The result is a hodgepodge of programs loosely defined by inappropriate, nonscientific terms such as *mental health problems, serious emotional disturbance, juvenile delinquency, criminal activities,* and so on.

In fact, institutional programs and policies must be reshaped accord-ing to a *scientifically* accurate classification system. Such a classification system for severely disabled children should include at least two very dif-ferent groups: (1) children with scientifically defined neurobiological dis-orders as listed above, which are biologically based brain disorders, and (2) children with "mental health" or psychological problems, which are sociologically or environmentally caused problems due, for example, to abuse, neglect, poverty, crime, alcohol and substance abuse, and neurotic, emotional, or life-adjustment issues.

Some children with severe disabilities will have elements of both an NBD and a mental health problem; an example would be a child with bipolar disorder who is abused. It is also understood that some children will have severe disabilities of as yet unknown etiology.

All severely disabled children need—and deserve to have—proper care and support. However, all institutions must develop *specific* and *effective* programs for *each* of these groups. It is illogical and scientifically unacceptable to apply the *same* programs and policies to all severely disabled children. Proper classification must be based on the latest scientific evidence and must adapt and change as new neurobiological discoveries are made.

Need for Special Education Programs

The crucial role of special education cannot be overstated for children severely disabled by a neurobiological disorder. Ideally, each state should offer a menu of educational programs for all disabled students that includes a mainstream setting, a resource room, a self-contained classroom, and a *variety* of special education schools. Then parents, educators, and physicians could select a program based on a child's individual needs.

For some students with an NBD, a mainstream or resource room setting with support services as needed may be sufficient. However, for students seriously disabled by the symptoms of their chronic NBD, a special education school is essential.

Unfortunately, many states have no special education schools for children and adolescents with an NBD and must send their most disabled children out of state for their education. Worse, some states and many school districts simply refuse to support such special programs. It is *essential* that all fifty states—and all school districts—have access to, and support, special education services for children severely disabled by an NBD.

Need for Specialists in Neurobiological Disorders in Children and Adolescents

As scientific knowledge increased in general medicine, subspecialties such as cardiology, urology, gastroenterology, infectious diseases, and so on developed. Unfortunately, child psychiatry has been very slow to develop a subspecialty in neurobiological disorders that would integrate the scientific revolution into daily practice. Even today, many child psychiatrists do not prescribe neurotropic medications for severe NBD or are not expert—or even trained—in using these drugs. In addition, many hospitals and clinics use a variety of "milieu therapies" or behavior modification techniques universally, without regard to the individual child's diagnosis (or classification, as discussed above), and without any long-term data demonstrating the efficacy of these approaches for children and youth with an NBD.

Why has progress been so slow? Here are some of the reasons: (1) Some child psychiatrists were trained in the preneuroscientific era and have little or no knowledge of the latest scientific findings. (2) Some physicians simply choose to ignore the neurobiological revolution. (3) Although many child psychiatrists have been trained in the biological basis of severe NBD, many refuse to treat patients with NBD. (4) Many psychiatric training programs still teach nonscientific approaches such as psychoanalysis and psychodynamic modalities as though they were equal in importance to scientifically based therapies (Detre, 1989). (5) Most important, there is a scarcity of full-time academic child psychiatrists who devote 80 percent or more of their time to scientific or clinical research in child and adolescent psychiatry or both (Institute of Medicine, 1989).

The current scientific evidence defining NBD now demands the creation of a new subspecialty of physician-scientists within child psychiatry. These NBD physician-scientists would (1) direct 100 percent of their research and clinical efforts to the treatment of severe NBD; (2) establish treatment programs for NBD that are based only on rigorous clinical trials and scientific data, and not on opinion and theory; (3) be expert in using the most effective psychopharmacological agents; and (4) treat patients and their caring families the way that doctors treat patients and families when a child has any other serious chronic disease such as diabetes or lupus.

Integration of the Neuroscience Revolution into Daily Practice

Until our society completely integrates the newest neurobiological data into the institutions charged with the care of children and adolescents, caring family members, parents, and interested professionals can take some specific and simple steps.

First, all of us can insist that psychiatric treatment must be based on science, empirical evidence, and efficacy, instead of on belief and theory. Some questions that psychiatric professionals should be required to answer are the following: Is the proposed treatment based on controlled scientific trials, or only on opinion and theory? What data are available about the treatment being recommended? What are the results of long-term follow-up studies? What scientific evidence is there that the treatment program has worked, or has a good probability of working?

Second, it is time to demand that clinical therapy in child psychiatry be held to the same scientific standards as the rest of medicine. These scientific standards have established a strict hierarchy to judge the value of three different kinds of clinical data to support the efficacy of a mode of therapy: (1) The prospective randomized trial is the most scientific evidence to support clinical treatment. This kind of trial is planned in advance to test the efficacy of a new form of therapy and is compared to a control group, which usually receives no treatment. The medical community has universally accepted the prospective clinical trial as the strongest evidence in support of a specific type of treatment. (2) Retrospective clinical data generally derive from studies reviewing the long-term effects of a specific therapy on a large number of patients. These studies are not as scientifically valid as prospective clinical trials. However, if several long-term retrospective studies show the same result, this information suggests that a particular treatment may be beneficial. (3) *Anecdotal data,* which consist of one or a few "case histories" or observations about one or several patients, are the least accepted kind of information in the medical community for demonstrating the efficacy of treatment.

Many of the psychopharmacological agents used today to treat NBD have been subjected to the rigorous, scientific scrutiny of prospective clinical trials. Unfortunately, many of the nonpharmacological forms of clinical therapy in child psychiatry have *not* been investigated scientifically. Instead, they rely almost exclusively on anecdotal data or on belief and theory. The treatment of NBD by child psychiatry must be based on the same scientific principles as other areas of clinical medicine. Anecdote and theory are insufficient to establish efficacy.

References

Detre, T. "Some Comments on the Future of Child and Adolescent Psychiatry." *Academic Psychiatry,* 1989, *13,* 189–195.

Institute of Medicine. *Research on Children and Adolescents with Mental, Behavioral, and Developmental Disorders.* Publication no. IOM-89-07. Washington, D.C.: National Academy Press, 1989.

Additional Sources

Andreasen, N. C. *The Broken Brain: The Biological Revolution in Psychiatry.* New York: Harper & Row, 1984.

Brain Research: The Journal of the California Alliance for the Mentally Ill, 1991, 2 (entire issue 4).

McElroy, E. *Children and Adolescents with Mental Illness: A Parents' Guide.* Kensington, Md.: Woodbine House, 1988.

Meltzer, H. Y. (ed.), in association with the American College of Neuropsychopharmacology. *Psychopharmacology: The Third Generation of Progress.* New York: Raven Press, 1987.

Peschel, E., and Peschel, R. "Adolescents with Biologically-Based Brain Disease—Professional Response and Support." *Connections: Newsletter of the National Center for Youth with Disabilities* (University of Minnesota), 1990, *1* (4), 1–4.

Peschel, E., and Peschel, R. "Science, Evidence, and Efficacy." *NAMI CAN News,* 1991, *1* (1), 1.

Peschel, R., and Peschel, E. "The Need for Specialists in Biologically-Based Brain Diseases." *Perceptual and Motor Skills,* 1990, *70,* 623–625.

Peschel, R., and Peschel, E. "Appropriate Classification Must Follow Scientific Discovery." *NAMI CAN News,* 1991, *1* (4), 1-2.

Peschel, R., and Peschel, E. "A Medical Model for Incorporating the Neuroscience Revolution into Child and Adolescent Psychiatry." *Decade of the Brain,* 1991, 2 (1), 6-7.

Peschel, R., and Peschel, E. "A Medical Model for Specialists in Biologically-Based Brain Disease." *Perceptual and Motor Skills,* 1991, 72, 96-98.

Peschel, R., and Peschel, E. "The Physician-Scientist in Child and Adolescent Psychiatry." *NAMI CAN News,* 1991, *1* (3), 1-2.

Peschel, R., and Peschel, E. "Prospective, Retrospective, and Anecdotal Data: A Demand for Science in Child Psychiatry." *NAMI CAN News,* 1991, *1* (2), 1-2.

Snyder, S. H. *Drugs and the Brain.* New York: Scientific American Library, 1986.

RICHARD PESCHEL *is professor of therapeutic radiology at Yale University School of Medicine.*

ENID PESCHEL *is co-director of the Program for Humanities in Medicine and assistant professor (adjunct) of internal medicine at Yale University School of Medicine.*

Highly individualized "wrap-around" services are emerging as viable alternatives to traditional categorical forms of treatment.

Individualized Services for Children

John E. VanDenBerg

Until recently, children suffering from neurobiological disorders (NBD) had few services options other than the "fifty-minute hour" or psychiatric hospitalization. As a result of federal initiatives over the last eight years, some states developed, as alternatives to the standard outpatient and inpatient services, what they called a "system of care" focused on the interagency development of case management, respite services, day treatment, therapeutic foster care, and other services (Stroul and Friedman, 1986). These services were categorical (based on categories): they represented preconceived service models into which children and families were brought for services.

In some states, however, even these improvements in available services alternatives did not have an effect on the most disabled youth in each state, who were still being institutionalized or otherwise inappropriately served. Typically, these children were those with an NBD, who were often not accepted into the new "system of care" services or who were quickly rejected from categorical services. One state in this situation—Alaska—eventually sought successful solutions by developing wrap-around or individualized services with consultation from the Kaleidoscope program in Chicago in an effort called the *Alaska Youth Initiative (AYI)*.

New Model of Services: Individualized Services

In the traditional "categorical" model of services, children are brought into preexisting programs and intervention models (Burchard and Clarke, 1990). When their needs are not met, they are often referred elsewhere, or they may be inadequately served. In an "individualized" model of services, however, an interdisciplinary team of persons (including the parents) first asks the question "What does this child need so that he or she can get better?" The team looks not only at medical issues but also at family and friends and vocational, educational, psychological, safety, economic, and other areas of need. The team agrees that it will offer the child unconditional care. This means that if the youth's needs are not met, the youth's individualized program will be changed and the youth cannot be "kicked out" when he or she exhibits the very disabilities that led to the need for services in the first place.

Wrap-around or individualized services are defined as interventions that are developed and approved by an interdisciplinary services team and that include delivery of individualized services in three or more life-domain areas of a child and family. An *interdisciplinary services team* is one that includes, at a minimum, the parents or legal guardian, the teacher or the vocational counselor or both, the therapist, the psychiatrist, and a services coordinator. In addition, the team may include the child, if appropriate; an advocate of the parents or the child or both; and any other person influential in the child's life, such as a neighbor or a friend.

Needs-based individualized services are built on the specific needs of the child and family and not on the availability of a particular categorical service. "Needs" are defined in positive terms, such as the need of a child to do art or to excel in school. *Life-domain needs* are areas of need that are defined by basic human needs that almost everyone experiences. These are (1) residential (a place to live); (2) family or surrogate family; (3) social (friends and contact with other people); (4) educational/vocational; (5) medical; (6) psychological/emotional; (7) legal (especially for children and youth with juvenile justice needs); (8) safety (the need to be safe); and (9) other child-specific life-domain areas, such as cultural and ethnic needs or community needs.

Through use of the individualized model of services, the Alaska effort successfully returned and served almost all of the children who had been placed out of state and has, over a six-year period, prevented many other youth from being inappropriately institutionalized. These improved services have *cost at least 37 percent less* than the previous categorical services (Alaska Department of Health and Social Services, 1991). Variations on the services model developed in Illinois and Alaska have been initiated in many places in the United States over the last several years.

Primary Lessons Learned from the Alaska Youth Initiative

The following are some important points for parents of children with neurobiological disorders.

The More Disabled the Child, the More Individualized the Services Need to Be. Categorical services are efficient in that large numbers of children can be served at one time, and the services are generally easier to manage. However, the more disabled the child, the more individualized the services need to be. Unfortunately, when children with NBD cannot benefit from categorical services, these children are often put into more restrictive and more categorical services, instead of being put into more individualized services. *Parents should advocate for highly individualized services when their child is not benefiting from a categorical service.*

When the Adults Agree, the Child Succeeds. After five years of AYI, there were no exceptions to this lesson. Frequently, categorical services are operated without extensive interagency involvement. Services are often determined by which serving agency (school, child welfare, mental health, and so on) ends up with primary responsibility for the child. However, with needs-based individualized services, all the important adults, regardless of their agency, must work together to *create* and *manage* services. Noncoordinated, highly categorical services often only meet the needs of the agency—not the needs of the child and caring family. *Parents should not accept the position of agencies that say "We don't work that way" or "It's too complicated" to work with other agencies.* What agency staff are really saying in these situations is that "We don't have time to do effective services" or "We're committed to an intervention model rather than to helping your child by changing our approaches."

When the Child's Needs Are Met, the Child Succeeds. Again, after five years of AYI, there were no exceptions to this lesson. The key to successful individualized services is good initial and *always ongoing assessment* of the child's needs and the family's needs. If key needs are not met due to inconvenience to the team or fallacious roadblocks such as "confidentiality," the child will rarely succeed. For example, if a fifteen-year-old's need to have friends is not met, it is likely that he or she will not stabilize. Even if a friend has to be hired, the need must be met. *Parents should strongly advocate for individualized interventions that address all of their child's needs, not just the needs that match the availability of services or the team's limited vision.*

"Unconditional Care" Is Crucial. The team makes an unconditional commitment to the child and family: this means that when the child's needs change, services will be modified and the child will not be expelled from the program. In AYI, this commitment was kept. No team gave up on the children, regardless of the severity of their disabilities. *Parents should demand unconditional care, not conditional care that is based on a theoretical model or the provider's convenience.*

Dollars Must Follow the Child. Categorical services are commonly based on rigid funding patterns. With individualized services, funding must be flexible and available for use by the team to meet the child's evolving needs. Often, not only do agencies fail to allow creative, flexible use of services dollars, but they also profess concerns about "accountability." In fact, of course, accountability should mean the *effectiveness of the service* and not the ease of fiscal tracking. Clearly, the AYI experience has shown that funds can follow the child and family and that accountability for the funds can remain high (Alaska Department of Health and Social Services, 1991). *Parents should demand that funds be made flexible, even if governmental fiscal policies must be changed.*

Summary

In Alaska, the development of a model of individualized services has been beneficial to children with neurobiological disorders. The AYI program has successfully demonstrated that even the most disabled children can be served in communities. This finding promotes a new level of less restrictive and more therapeutic alternatives tailored to the needs of children and their caring families.

References

Alaska Department of Health and Social Services. *The Alaska Youth Initiative Annual Report.* Juneau, Alaska: Alaska Department of Health and Social Services, 1991.

Burchard, J. D., and Clarke, R. T. "The Role of Individualized Care in a Service Delivery System for Children and Adolescents with Severely Maladjusted Behavior." *Journal of Mental Health Administration,* 1990, 17 (1), 48–60.

Stroul, B. A., and Friedman, R. *A System of Care for Severely Emotionally Disturbed Children and Youth.* Washington, D.C.: Georgetown University Child Development Center, 1986.

JOHN E. VANDENBERG, *director of the Pressley Ridge Center for Research and Public Policy in Pittsburgh, Pennsylvania, is the former coordinator of Child and Adolescent Mental Health Services for the State of Alaska.*

As Congress and the states consider sweeping reform of our health care system, citizen advocacy to ensure adequate insurance coverage for neurobiological disorders is vital.

Reforming Insurance Law to Provide Equitable Coverage for Persons with Neurobiological Disorders

Anne Marie O'Keefe

Parents whose child or adolescent has one of the neurobiological disorders (NBD) called "mental" illness soon learn how unprotected they are in terms of medical insurance. As the bills come in, they discover that serious "mental" illness is one disease that can easily drive them into bankruptcy. Whereas their health policy may pay 80 or 90 percent of the cost of other diseases, it may pay only 50 percent of the cost of "mental" illness. Whereas a policy has unlimited coverage or coverage up to $1 million for heart disease or other catastrophic illnesses, it may have a $10,000 lifetime limit for "mental" illness or an arbitrary annual limit of $500. This is totally inadequate for a serious brain disease that must be carefully managed for the rest of the patient's life.

A Historical Perspective

At the end of the nineteenth century, it was suspected that serious mental illness was biologically based. But as long as the neurosciences remained primitive, the best treatments for the severely "mentally" ill were decent food and housing and a supportive milieu. Not until 1955 were the first drugs discovered that controlled symptoms of some NBD. Now, more recent discoveries have established that many "mental" illnesses are biologically based brain diseases.

Unfortunately, under existing insurance law, the treatment of these devastating physical diseases is grouped with various psychotherapies that do not treat physical disease but are aimed at improving a client's personal insight. Thus, most insurance policies give people with serious NBD the same coverage as healthy people who have transitory problems in living.

Proper treatment can help many people with NBD lead productive lives, yet only a small minority of these people now receives adequate care. If people seriously ill with NBD and those who only have problems in living have the same levels of insurance coverage, it is more financially rewarding for providers to help those with minor emotional problems. It is also easier to treat people with transitory adjustment problems than to tackle the long-term problems of persons with chronic brain disease. The increase in providers and consumers of psychotherapy and the popular desire to have such services covered by insurance policies have led to a trade-off made at the expense of people with serious chronic NBD. In the current maze of state regulation of insurance policies, coverage to treat mental and emotional problems is generally very broad but very shallow. "Mental health" benefits, which include the treatment of serious mental illness (NBD), have low levels of reimbursement, high copayments, and very low annual and lifetime limits. Such limits have been imposed because counseling for emotional problems is subject to what insurance companies call *moral hazard:* the fact that people overuse discretionary services when they get them for little or no money (McGuire, 1989). Moral hazard is high in the area of mental health care because psychotherapy is very "price sensitive": when consumers must pay for it, they do not buy much of it, but if they can get it at low cost, they use it a lot.

Insurance Coverage

Unfortunately, people with serious chronic NBD cannot choose whether or not to receive treatment. Treatment for such people can mean the difference between life and death. Yet people with NBD are subject to the same limits designed to control the overuse of discretionary mental health services by healthy people. This current state of affairs is highly discriminatory. Simply because an NBD attacks the brain instead of the liver or heart, families face financial ruin when a child or other family member develops an NBD. For example, of all health insurance plans covering federal workers, the average beneficiary pays only $2,500 out of pocket for a physical illness costing $100,000. Yet for a "mental" illness with the same price tag, fully insured families in the federal program pay from $25,000 to $75,000 out of pocket (Hustead and others, 1985). Very few federal workers can afford this kind of money. Nor should they have to.

Insurance companies say that costs for mental and emotional problems are uncontrollable. Yet recent studies show very low prevalence rates for such NBD as schizophrenia and bipolar and major depressive disorders (Regier and others, 1988). Statistics from the Civilian Health and Medical Program of the Uniformed Services (1990) show that at any given time, less than 1 percent of its insured population is being treated for these serious "mental" illnesses.

NBD are serious—but very rare—disorders. Thus, the cost of adequately covering NBD is low. In March 1991, the Coopers & Lybrand accounting firm, commissioned by the California Medical Association Access to Better Care Task Force, calculated the financial implications of extending unlimited inpatient and outpatient coverage for the treatment of schizophrenia, bipolar disorder, autism, and pervasive developmental disorders. This extension of coverage would treat these serious "mental" illnesses the same as other physical diseases included under the major medical benefit. Coopers & Lybrand concluded that the cost of extending unlimited coverage for these specific NBD would total only $0.78 per month per insured person. To achieve this increase at only $0.78 per month per insured person would require at least two million people in the insurance pool to control for adverse selection.

If fairness and equitable treatment are not compelling enough arguments, and if compassion for persons with a devastating disease is not enough to change the existing laws to cover NBD on a par with other serious physical illnesses, consider the results. It now costs over $25,000 per year to keep one person in jail. According to professionals who have worked at the Los Angeles County Jail, approximately 15 percent of the inmates—about 3,600 persons—have "serious mental illnesses." This makes the Los Angeles County Jail "the largest mental hospital in this country" (Torrey, Erdman, Wolfe, and Flynn, 1991, p. 6). Some experts estimate about 10 percent of all prisoners in the United States—around 100,000 people—have schizophrenia or manic-depressive psychosis (Torrey, Erdman, Wolfe, and Flynn, 1990, p. 6). Proper insurance coverage for serious NBD could save much of this wasted expenditure. More expensive than its financial toll is what insurance discrimination costs in terms of human suffering. One of the most heartbreaking results of our nation's discrimination against persons with NBD is the legions of homeless "mentally" ill. There is a reasonable consensus that about one-third of the homeless population suffers from serious NBD (Torrey, 1988, p. 7). For these persons, health insurance is the first of many failed safety nets.

By discriminating against people with serious NBD in health policies, we shift the cost away from private health insurers and onto the public sector. When we make this choice, we multiply the total price tag many times, increase the human suffering that results, and waste the lives of many innocent people.

Citizen Advocacy

The best hope to achieve insurance equity for NBD is citizen advocacy. Most laws that govern insurance are on the state level, and well-organized citizen coalitions have already changed the laws in some states. California passed the first of these antidiscrimination laws (California Assembly Bill 1692, 1989). Since January 1990, all insurers in California who offer group policies on a group basis have been required to offer coverage for "schizophrenia, schizo-affective disorder, bipolar and delusional depressions, and pervasive developmental disorder" on the same basis as "other disorders of the brain."

In 1991, Texas passed a law that prohibits insurance discrimination against persons with "serious mental illness," including schizophrenia, paranoid and other psychotic disorders, bipolar disorders, major depressive disorders, and schizo-affective disorders, in all policies sold to state workers (Texas H.B. 2, Sections 11.106–11.112, June 6, 1991). This was achieved by amending the part of the state insurance code prohibiting discrimination against persons with AIDS. As this volume goes to press, several other states are considering similar measures.

Persons interested in achieving social reform should build on these important beginnings. Citizen advocates will quickly discover that state legislators are responsive to their constituents' needs and desires. When framed in terms of equity, fairness, and economic good sense, the arguments for parity coverage of neurobiological disorders are very compelling. But to be successful, advocates must be willing to work hard over long periods of time (O'Keefe, 1991).

References

California Assembly Bill 1692, 1989. Added to Section 10123.15 of the California Insurance Code, "Disability Insurance: Serious Mental Illness."

Civilian Health and Medical Program of the Uniformed Services. *CHAMPUS Annual Mental Health Reports 1990.* Aurora, Colo.: Civilian Health and Medical Program of the Uniformed Services, 1990.

Hustead, E., Sharfstein, S. S., Muszynski, M., Brady, J., and Cahill, J. "Reductions in Coverage for Mental and Nervous Illness in Federal Employees' Health Benefits Program, 1980-84." *American Journal of Psychiatry,* 1985, *142* (2), 181–186.

McGuire, T. G. "Financing and Reimbursement of Mental Health Services." In C. Taube and D. Mechanic (eds.), *The Future of Mental Health Services Research.* Washington, D.C.: National Institute of Mental Health, 1989.

O'Keefe, A. M. *Handbook for Advocating Insurance Reform.* Arlington, Va.: National Alliance for the Mentally Ill, 1991.

Regier, D. A., Boyd, J. H., Burke, J. D., Rae, D. S., Myers, J. K., Kramer, M., Robins, L. N., George, L. K., Karno, M., and Locke, B. Z. "One-Month Prevalence of Mental Disorders in the United States." *Archives of General Psychiatry,* 1988, *45,* 977–986.

Torrey, E. F. *Nowhere to Go: The Tragic Odyssey of the Homeless Mentally Ill.* New York: Harper-Collins, 1988.

Torrey, E. F., Erdman, K., Wolfe, S. M., and Flynn, L. M. *Care of the Seriously Mentally Ill.* Washington, D.C.: Public Citizen Health Research Group and National Alliance for the Mentally Ill, 1990.

ANNE MARIE O'KEEFE, health care psychologist and attorney, is vice president for health issues at The Kamber Group in Washington, D.C.

The 1987 case of Arkansas Blue Cross and Blue Shield, Inc. v.
Jane Doe is a blueprint of a successful legal case documenting that
bipolar disorder is a biological and physical illness that the
insurance industry should cover on a par with other physical
illnesses.

Obtaining Insurance Coverage for Bipolar Disorder and Other Neurobiological Disorders on a Par with Other Physical Illnesses

Donald M. Spears

"You have no insurance coverage because your son has a mental illness."

I recall the helplessness that my wife and I felt hearing those words, plus our fear that denial of coverage meant that our son would not be able to get adequate, urgently needed medical care. We were further shocked to learn that the same scenario was being replayed daily for other caring families all over the United States. As an attorney, I decided to challenge the system.

Our son's first hospitalization was short and resulted in a diagnosis of bipolar disorder (BD). We learned that BD is biological and physical in nature but manifests itself with symptoms of "mental" illness, including aberrant thoughts, emotional reactions, and behaviors. We educated ourselves about the nature and origins of BD. It became clear to me that an insurance policy's declaration that it does not provide coverage for "nervous and mental disorders"—and does not define the disorders so excluded—is susceptible to abuse by an insurance company that wants to avoid coverage for a chronic illness. How does one challenge this?

A Landmark Case

To approach an insurance carrier, you must be able to establish the biological and physical nature of the disorder for which you are trying to obtain coverage. Recent neuroscience and basic science research have docu-

NEW DIRECTIONS FOR MENTAL HEALTH SERVICES, no. 54, Summer 1992 © Jossey-Bass Publishers

mented that many disorders called "mental" disorders are, in fact, biologically based disorders: neurobiological disorders (NBD). (See Part One.) But historically, the psychiatric profession has categorized the illnesses it treats by symptoms instead of by cause. It is this classification of disorders by symptoms that most often creates problems in obtaining insurance coverage for NBD. In the medical and insurance industry, the standard for classification is the *diagnosis related group* (DRG). When making a diagnosis, a doctor refers to that diagnosis via DRG section. Thus NBD, which are physical in nature, fall under a DRG that categorizes them as "mental," because of the symptoms manifested.

Once you have educated yourself about your child's NBD and can argue persuasively that this particular NBD is biological and physical in nature, you must step into the arena of law. While doing legal research on my son's illness, I was fortunate enough to find an Arkansas Court of Appeals case, *Arkansas Blue Cross and Blue Shield, Inc. v. Jane Doe* (1987). If there is a landmark decision in regard to establishing the rationale for insurance coverage for an NBD, it is this case. It evolved around the plaintiff Jane Doe, an adolescent diagnosed with BD, who had been treated medically with success. But when Jane Doe's medical and hospital bills were submitted, her insurance carrier denied payment, except for a limited amount of coverage, because, it claimed, her expenses were incurred as a result of an alleged "mental" condition.

The evidence presented by Jane Doe's attorney is a classic example of how to establish the burden of proof necessary to prevail in such a case. The evidence consisted of testimony from several individuals who established Jane Doe's history, including the problems she had had before she was diagnosed with BD and obtained treatment. After her history was presented, her attorney placed into evidence testimony that this adolescent had been treated with medications known to be effective for BD and that she had responded positively to them. The plaintiff then introduced testimony of various mental health professionals who indicated that "those of the medical profession who dealt in mental conditions had historically categorized these illnesses by symptom rather than cause" (*Arkansas Blue Cross,* 1987, p. 431). The testimony further established that competent psychiatry now classifies illness by cause or origin, rather than by symptom, and that the overwhelming weight of medical research now shows that BD is a physical disorder. The professional witnesses for the plaintiff then zeroed in on the DRG method of classification, stating basically that DRG was a "primitive way of classification and the profession was moving away from that method" (*Arkansas Blue Cross,* 1987, p. 431).

In its findings, the trial court held that BD was a physical condition and, as such, should be covered under the terms of the Arkansas Blue Cross and Blue Shield policy. The court further found that "classification of illnesses by symptom rather than cause was falling into disfavor within the mental health profession, and a large number of physicians and people in psychiatry were now classifying illnesses by their cause or origin" (*Arkansas Blue Cross*, 1987, p. 432).

One of the court's key findings, which relates to obtaining insurance coverage for other NBD, was that "classification manuals used by physicians, hospitals, and medical insurers would not be controlling on this issue [mental versus physical condition] because they were not adopted in, referred to, or made a part of the policy" (*Arkansas Blue Cross*, 1987, p. 432). Thus, the court found in this case that merely because the DRG of an illness may call it a "mental" condition, that classification was not necessarily the controlling determination on which denial of coverage could be based if, in fact, the underlying causes of the disorder were of a physical nature.

This landmark case was well developed and well tried, and the logic of the trial court in rendering its decision was based on current scientific evidence and common sense.

A Blueprint—and a Victory

Here is a possible blueprint for families to use in approaching an insurance company to obtain coverage under an existing policy for an NBD: (1) Surround yourself with competent psychiatric professionals who understand the origins and causes of NBD and will testify that the condition in question is physical in nature. (2) Provide the insurance company with the patient's complete history, documented by experts. This is essential. Documentation should set out that the individual has responded favorably to medical treatment or that failure to obtain medical treatment will create a danger to the health and welfare of the patient and those around him or her, in which case the insurance carrier might have greater liability than mere nonpayment of medical expenses. (3) Get an understanding of the present status of the law in your jurisdiction. The Jane Doe case was an Arkansas case; as such, that case is not controlling in other jurisdictions. However, the Arkansas Jane Doe case should be presented to your attorney for review because the reasoning in that case applies to all NBD conditions, regardless of the jurisdiction in which the affected individual lives. (4) To select an attorney, one should understand that this is a newly developing area of the law. Unless an attorney has personal experience because of a family member's illness or has litigated in this area, most attorneys will not be conversant with the issues involved in NBD insurance litigation. (5) Last, and probably most important in a successful pursuit of insurance coverage, is persistence. You will receive more than one denial from your insurance carrier. Denial does not necessarily mean that coverage is not available; it just means that the insurance carrier is interpreting the policy conditions in the light most favorable to the company. The current situation is the result of narrow, uninformed, and uneducated interpretations of policy exclusions for "nervous and mental disorders."

My personal experience in pursuing coverage on behalf of my son was successful. My family carried two major medical policies: one provided a $75,000 per condition coverage, the other, a $1 million per condition coverage, with a $25,000 deductible. I pursued the course laid out above. The company that held the $75,000 major medical coverage paid the entire sum, without the necessity of litigation. When I tried to resolve coverage with the other carrier, I was unable to do so without resorting to litigation. After the suit was filed against the insurance company and the discovery process was commenced, I presented to the carrier the evidentiary base that I set out above. After about eight months of litigation, we entered into a settlement agreement. It provided that the carrier would pay for my son's treatment as a covered illness under the policy, for the full amount provided in the policy.

Regardless of the jurisdiction in which you are located, you may obtain relief under most medical policies for a diagnosis of BD. Coverage should also be available for other NBD, but that coverage must be pursued with persistence.

Reference

Arkansas Blue Cross and Blue Shield, Inc. v. Jane Doe, 22 Ark. App. 89, 733 S.W. 2d 429 (1987).

DONALD M. SPEARS is an attorney in Malvern, Arkansas.

*In many states, competent, caring parents must declare themselves
"unfit," often before a judge, and surrender custody of their child
with a neurobiological disorder so that their child can receive state-
funded medical care, which the parents cannot afford.*

Parents Forced to Surrender Custody of Children with Neurobiological Disorders

Cecile L. Ervin

Part One of this volume documents the neurobiological basis of the severe disabilities from which children and adolescents with neurobiological disorders (NBD) suffer: persistent or intermittent behavioral, emotional, and cognitive disturbances. Some children with NBD may exhibit such behaviors as self-mutilation, violence, fire setting, very disruptive behaviors in school and home, threats and actual harm to parents and siblings, and violent rages and attempted suicide (communication with parents . . . , n.d.). In struggling to obtain proper diagnosis, treatment, and care for their children, parents exhaust their finances. This chapter examines what happens when parents must turn to the state to provide their child's treatment because they can no longer afford to do so. Procedures vary from state to state, but often, to obtain state funds, parents must use existing child welfare laws, be adjudicated "unfit" to provide care, and be required to relinquish custody of their child to the state. Parents are stigmatized in the process, and the family unit on which the child or youth with an NBD relies for support is undermined.

To understand why our society requires competent, caring parents to be labeled "unfit" before the state provides benefits to the child, we must examine the conditions under which the state may intervene in the parent-child relationship and the procedures it uses for that intervention. Under our laws, parents have substantial authority to rear their children and regulate their behavior as they see fit. For example, we allow parents to discipline their own children. But if that discipline crosses an arbitrary line defined by our laws and becomes abusive, the state, through its child protective services, will intercede to protect the child. Using child welfare procedures, the state will try to reeducate the parents, place the child in foster care, or even terminate the parent-child relationship if the state determines that it is in the child's best interest. The strong presumption of family unity is rebutted by harm to the child. However, the frequent failure of agencies to protect and to serve children once they enter the system is well documented (Greene, 1990; Lyon, 1987; Weithorn, 1988). Among the problems are lack of coordination of services from one agency to another and improper admission, diagnostic, and treatment criteria (Soler and Shauffer, 1990; Weithorn, 1988; Zenoff and Zients, 1983).

Currently, because there are no laws specifically designed for children with NBD, the child welfare laws designed to protect abused and neglected children are applied, out of context and often out of convenience, to children with NBD and to their families. Parent and child are labeled in the language of the welfare laws as "unfit" parent and "neglected" child. Once the parents have surrendered custody, the child is placed in a state facility. The "unfit" label may be used to prevent parents from participating in decisions about their child's treatment and even from seeing their child for extended periods of time. At times, parents even lose custody of their children permanently (McManus and Friesen, 1989; composite of personal communications with parents who have relinquished custody to the state, n.d.).

A Case in Point

A case that went to federal court in New York in 1982 illustrates the process. Parents whose "emotionally disturbed" children needed treatment and supervision that the parents could not afford asked the State of New York to provide care. (These children were not identified as having NBD, but the process would still apply.) Under the state's application of child welfare statutes, parents were required to relinquish custody of their child to the state prior to obtaining care, even though nowhere in the law was transfer of custody the exclusive means of admission to a state residential treatment facility at state expense (*Joyner v. Dumpson*, 1982). The relinquishment process consisted of two steps: (1) Parents and the local social service agency signed a voluntary placement agreement (VPA) transferring custody of the child to the agency providing the service. By signing that agreement, parents affirmed that they were unable to adequately support, maintain, and supervise their child at home. (2) If the social worker believed that the child would be in the facility more than thirty days, he or she was required to petition the family court judge to approve the custody transfer. Although this transfer process did not require parents to stand up in court and claim themselves "unfit," as is required in many jurisdictions, the effects were often the same. The judge had to be satisfied that the parents voluntarily signed the VPA, that transfer served the "best interest" of the child, and that it was contrary to the child's welfare to remain in the home.

The lower court found that the statute interfered with the parents' fundamental right to rear and retain custody of their child. On appeal, the higher court said that the transfer requirement did not infringe on the parents' right to privacy because the parents *voluntarily* decided to place the child in state custody (*Joyner* v. *Dumpson,* 1983). It should be pointed out that parents voluntarily accepted transfer because they were financially unable to do otherwise. Parents' rights were arguably abridged (although the court did not so find) because (1) the return of the child was based on the state's determination of the parents' ability to care for the child; (2) the state retained the ultimate power to place the child, determine the medical treatment, and control visitation, no matter what powers the parents seemed to have under the VPA; and (3) the state had the ultimate power to isolate the child from his or her caring parents.

Funding: The Force Behind Custody Transfers

Why are custody transfers used to obtain long-term medical care for a child with an NBD? Often, after having spent years paying for medical treatment for their child or adolescent with a severe NBD, capable supportive parents have depleted their finances. Any insurance funds they once had are now exhausted. The private hospital treating their child has told them to take their child home, stating either that the child is better or that the hospital cannot provide further treatment without insurance. The parents learn that if they want their child to receive long-term medical treatment, they must pay $4,000 to $12,000 per month for the child's care in a residential treatment facility. Most parents cannot afford such a financial burden (communication with parents).

In Pennsylvania, for example, parents found that the cost of group home care for their seriously disturbed children ranged from $25,000 to $60,000 per year (Enda, 1990). Almost all state and federal money for such care was available only through the child welfare system, instead of the mental health system. Welfare system funds were only available to children in actual state custody (Enda, 1990). In Georgia in 1987, care for extremely disturbed youth averaged $80,000 per year. The Georgia Department of Human Resources (DHR) estimated that it needed $13.7 million to care for about 92,000 such youth, but the legislature allocated only $1.4 million. The DHR prioritized children in state custody to receive funded care first. Since children in parental custody were the lowest funding priority, parents relinquished custody to the state so that their child could receive medical treatment (Hansen, 1987).

In testimony before the U.S. House of Representatives Committee on Ways and Means, McManus and Friesen (1989) addressed why "in countless instances" parents of children with severe "emotional" illnesses have surrendered custody for state-provided care: (1) State officials mistakenly believe that federal funds under Title IV-E of the Social Security Act are only available when the state has custody of the child. (2) State agencies prefer the *convenience* of simplified procedures: they do not have to work with parents who have lost custody of their child. McManus and Friesen (1989, p. 1) emphasized that the parents would *not* have relinquished custody to the state *if* they had been able to afford their child's treatment, nor would the state have considered taking legal custody *if* the state were not providing funds. In other words, the parents were only adjudicated "unfit" because they cared enough to want their severely ill child to receive medical treatment, which they could not afford.

Pervasiveness of the Transfer-of-Custody Problem

In a nonrandom sample survey of 966 parents whose children needed long-term care, 25 percent of the parents indicated that someone had suggested that they transfer custody of their child to the state in order for the child's treatment to be funded. One-third of that 25 percent had actually transferred custody to the state (McManus and Friesen, 1989).

A study by Cohen, Harris, Gottlieb, and Best (1991) of 117 agencies in forty-five responding states reported that 32 percent of the agencies indicated that they had used custody transfer to get state funding for a child's treatment. Sixty-seven percent of the agencies that had used custody transfer were juvenile correctional institutions, 61 percent were social service agencies, 42 percent were youth service agencies, and only 17 percent were mental health agencies. But in fact, use of custody transfer was probably underestimated because, Cohen's group discovered, 11 percent of the parents who reported that they had transferred custody did so in states where agencies had reported that transfers did *not* occur.

In 1990, studies indicated that 500,000 children in the United States were in state custody; it is estimated that 850,000 will be in state custody by 1995 (Greene, 1990). In 1987, 340,000 children were in state foster homes (70 percent), about 92,000 (19 percent) in detention facilities, and about 55,000 (11 percent) in residential care for "emotional" problems (Greene, 1990, pp. 2–3). The *Invisible Child* study indicated that mental health agencies represented only 9 percent of the agencies that had placed 4,000 children in out-of-state residential treatment facilities (National Mental Health Association, 1988). Thus, many more children with NBD are served by the child welfare and juvenile correction systems than by the mental health system. The number of children in state custody that have NBD is unknown. The number of parents that have had to transfer custody to receive state-funded care is also unknown.

Recommendations

Until our society provides adequate commitment of funds, consensus in diagnosis and treatment criteria, and coordination of agencies to provide services to the more than three million children *severely* disabled by some kinds of "mental disorder" (National Institute of Mental Health, 1990, p. 2), custody transfers via the state child welfare systems are likely to continue. Here are some guidelines to make maximum use of these systems.

Parents and professionals should thoroughly inform themselves about the nature of custody transfers in their jurisdiction. For example, does the law *require* custody transfer for funding—or is custody transfer merely the custom of a particular state agency? How will parents transfer custody— voluntarily, or by declaring themselves "unfit"? What happens to the ill child transferred to the state? Will the child be sent out of state? Who may effect a transfer to another facility? Who chooses the long-term care facility? Who will continually monitor and reevaluate the appropriateness and efficacy of the child's placement and treatment? What criteria determine length of custody?

Professionals should adequately inform parents of the nature of custody transfer and the impact it will have on the child and the entire family. For example, what happens if parents transfer custody? Do they relinquish custody temporarily—or lose custody permanently? Will parents be able to participate in treatment decisions affecting their own child? Will parents lose contact with their child? Who will diagnose the child's illness and plan the child's treatment? Can parents demand a reevaluation of their child's diagnosis and treatment? Who determines when the child can be reunited with his or her parents, and by what criteria?

Parents and professionals—including psychiatrists, nurses, psychologists, social workers, judges, lawyers, and child advocates—should work together to try to establish criteria for diagnosis, admission, and treatment of children with severe neurobiological disorders. Two specific recommendations to improve conditions are the following: (1) Establish a federally funded national computer data bank to amass, analyze, and synthesize needed information to determine the extent of the custody transfer problem and to provide information to reform the system. The data bank, which would include the latest scientific research and knowledge about NBD in children and adolescents, would also contain information gained from empirical evidence about the most effective treatments for NBD and methods of managed care. In all data collection, the utmost care would be necessary to protect the confidentiality and rights of patients and families. (2) Create a pilot program that will use the data obtained from the first step to establish a method of assessing an individual child's need for treatment and to design state or federally financed care for children with severe NBD that does *not* require resorting to laws written for abused and neglected children, for whom the child welfare system was designed.

Dedicated, devoted parents should not have to declare themselves "unfit" to receive state-assisted care for a child suffering from a severe NBD. Families and children can be protected and assisted as a unit in the child's "best interest" through a more scientifically based and equitable use of resources.

References

Cohen, R., Harris, R., Gottlieb, S., and Best, A. M. "States' Use of Transfer of Custody as a Requirement for Providing Services to Emotionally Disturbed Children." *Hospital and Community Psychiatry,* 1991, *42,* 526–530.

Enda, J. "A Question of Custody." *Philadelphia Inquirer,* Mar. 22, 1990, sec. I, p. 1.

Greene, K. E. "Mental Health Care for Children: Before and After State Custody." *Campbell Law Review,* 1990, *13* (1), 1–56.

Hansen, J. O. "Desperate to Get Care for Disturbed Children, Parents Give Them Up." *Atlanta Journal and Constitution,* June 26, 1987, p. 1A.

Joyner v. Dumpson, 533 F. Supp. 233 (S.D.N.Y. 1982), *rev'd* 712 F.2d 770 (2d Cir. 1983).

Lyon, R. "Speaking for a Child: The Role of Independent Counsel for Minors." *California Law Review,* 1987, *75,* 680–706.

McManus, M., and Friesen, B. J. *Relinquishing Legal Custody as a Means of Obtaining Services for Children Who Have Serious Mental or Emotional Disorders.* Testimony before Subcommittee on Human Resources, Committee on Ways and Means, U.S. House of Representatives, June 1, 1989.

National Institute of Mental Health. *National Plan for Research on Child and Adolescent Mental Disorders: A Report Requested by the U.S. Congress.* Department of Health and Human Services publication no. (ADM) 90-1683. Washington, D.C.: U.S. Government Printing Office, 1990.

National Mental Health Association. *Final Report and Recommendations of the Invisible Child Project.* Alexandria, Va.: National Mental Health Association, 1988.

Soler, M., and Shauffer, C. "Fighting Fragmentation: Coordination of Services for Children and Families." *Nebraska Law Review,* 1990, *69,* 278–297.

Weithorn, L. A. "Mental Hospitalization of Troublesome Youth: An Analysis of Skyrocketing Admission Rates." *Stanford Law Review,* 1988, *40,* 773–838.

Zenoff, E., and Zients, A. B. "If Civil Commitment for Children Is the Answer, What Are the Questions?" *George Washington Law Review,* 1983, *51* (2), 171–218.

CECILE L. ERVIN, *assistant professor of health law at the University of Texas Health Science Center at Houston, holds a joint appointment in the Family Practice and Community Medicine Department at the University of Texas Medical School.*

Advocates must fight inappropriate school decisions to obtain appropriate services.

A Free, Appropriate Public Education for Children with Neurobiological Disorders—Sometimes Available Only Through Due Process Litigation

Theodore A. Sussan

Due process litigation is sometimes necessary in order to provide a free, appropriate public education (FAPE) to children with neurobiological disorders. A few comments on recent Congressional and legal developments will be useful.

Legislative and Judicial Background

In 1975, Congress enacted the landmark Education of the Handicapped Act—Public Law 94-142—which, in conjunction with the Rehabilitation Act of 1973, mandated for the first time in the United States that children suffering certain handicapping conditions were entitled to a free, appropriate public education to meet their unique needs. On October 30, 1990, the act's name was changed to Individuals with Disabilities Education Act (IDEA) (United States Code Annotated, Title 20, Section 1400, 1990). Under IDEA, disabilities include mental retardation, hearing impairments, speech or language impairments, visual impairments, serious emotional disturbance, orthopedic impairments, autism, traumatic brain injury, and other health impairments or specific learning disabilities. Recent amendments also establish a new program of support for special education improvement projects and related services dealing with children with "serious emotional disturbance."

Children with disabilities have a right to an FAPE until June after their

NEW DIRECTIONS FOR MENTAL HEALTH SERVICES, no. 54, Summer 1992 © Jossey-Bass Publishers

twenty-first birthday. Section 1401, paragraph 18 of IDEA defines FAPE as "special education and related services that (A) have been provided at public expense, under public supervision and direction, and without charge, (B) meet the standards of the State education agency, (C) include an appropriate preschool, elementary, or secondary school education in the State involved, and (D) are provided in conformity with the individualized education program required under Section 1414 (a) (5) of this title."

The landmark Supreme Court case of *Rowley* v. *Board of Education* of the Hendrick Hudson School District (1982) further defines *appropriate* as meaning special education and related services that enable the pupil to materially benefit from his or her education. *Related services* are defined as meaning transportation, developmental, corrective, and other services as are required to assist a child with a disability in benefiting from special education. Related services may include counseling, psychotherapy, summer enrichment activities, occupational therapy, and so on. The federal office for special education has ruled that the appropriateness of related services must be determined on a case-by-case basis, according to the child's needs. Services that are strictly medical in nature and that can only be performed by a medical doctor are not considered related services that a school district must provide. A youngster's specific placement will depend on the needs involved and where those needs can best be met. Wherever appropriate educational progress can be made will represent the least restrictive environment.

Local school districts and their child-study teams (usually comprising a learning consultant, psychologist, and social worker) are charged with the responsibility of identifying and evaluating children with disabilities. Such children are given a "classification" that, from an educational perspective, attempts to accurately describe the disability. Unfortunately, many children with the neurobiological disorders (NBD) described in Part One of this volume are misclassified because IDEA does not have a category of NBD. As a result, these children often do *not* receive services appropriate to their NBD. The term *seriously emotionally disturbed (SED)* and the mental health term *emotional and behavioral disorders,* both of which are often applied to children with NBD, are inaccurate. Children with NBD have biologically based brain disorders, which are organic disorders.

Prerequisites to Litigation

Section 1415 of IDEA, "Procedural Safeguards," enumerates procedures that each state is required to make available, including record review, representation, prior notice before initiating change, conduct of the hearing itself, and rights of appeal. Therefore, the initial phase of any possible litigation must commence with obtaining and reviewing a complete copy of the pupil records.

Pupil records include not only the individualized education plans (IEP), but also evaluations by child-study teams, conference notes, anecdotal records, summaries of all meetings between team members, telephone logs, outside independent examinations, correspondence, records maintained by the nursing office, and the entire cumulative file. Advocates should not underestimate the significance of procedural infirmities because *failure to follow proper procedure could in and of itself be the equivalent of a denial of a FAPE.* Parents whose child requires special education should keep a complete file of their child's school, medical, and psychological records, plus evaluations by all consultants.

After the comprehensive review of pupil records, it is critical to obtain evaluations by experts that support the parents' position. Often, services of a qualified neurologist, psychiatrist, and learning consultant can effectively neutralize the testimony of the district's child-study team and persuade an administrative law judge that the conclusions of the school's child-study team are faulty. In effect, the parents, who are assembling their own child-study team, should coordinate each expert's testimony so that the team members can truly act as a team when testimony is given in court. Thus, the parents' team can arrive at a comprehensive, well-reasoned recommendation regarding issues of classification, program, and placement. No matter how well intentioned parents may be, without expert testimony, the odds of a successful outcome are seriously diminished.

School districts unfortunately base many of their conclusions on how a child acts, rather than on what *makes* a child act in a particular way. In other words, the "effect" is emphasized, with little or no thought given to the "cause." Many disabilities manifest themselves in similar ways, but effective treatment depends on accurate diagnosis. The effectiveness of a classification, program, and placement can only be as good as the accuracy of the initial diagnosis.

Federal law requires a speedy conclusion to due process cases, with a maximum time limit of forty-five days between the initial request and the final decision. Because of these accelerated time periods, an advocate should be prepared to be in trial before a judge within one to three weeks after the request for due process has been made. Therefore, it would be wise to have all expert reports in hand and witnesses' availability determined prior to requesting due process.

The due process trial takes place in a court-like setting in which witnesses are sworn to tell the truth and in which each side is presented with the opportunity to offer testimony and other evidence. Each witness is subject to both direct and cross-examination, all of which can be critical in producing a winning case.

Due process cases can last anywhere from a few days to several weeks, depending on the number of witnesses, the length of direct examination and cross-examination, and other factors. There is usually a direct relationship between the board of education's ultimate economic liability and the length of the case. The more it will cost, the more vigorous the contest.

The costs for counsel and expert witnesses can be significant. Prior to 1986, many parents were put in a position of literally having to mortgage their homes to fund due process litigation. This has been changed by what is known as the Attorney's Fee Bill. This law, effective August 6, 1986, states that whenever a parent prevails in a due process hearing, application for reasonable counsel fees and costs can be made against the local school district. Therefore, if parents hire an attorney to represent them in arbitration, mediation, or due process, and if, as a result of the attorney's efforts, the legal relationship between the parties has changed, the possibility of reimbursement for fees and costs exists. Several federal cases closely examine the Attorney's Fee Bill and what criteria courts consider in awarding fees (*Burpee* v. *Manchester School District,* 1987; *Michael F.* v. *Cambridge School Department,* 1987; *Rollison* v. *Biggs,* 1987).

Special education law is complex and procedurally intricate. An in-depth knowledge of disabled children's rights is a prerequisite for successfully bringing a local school district to due process with the ultimate goal of providing a FAPE.

Legal and Advocacy Organizations

Center for Law and Education, 236 Massachusetts Ave., N.E., #504, Washington, DC 20002.

Center for Law and Education, Inc., 955 Massachusetts Ave., #3A, Cambridge, MA 02139.

Children's Defense Fund, 122 C St., N.W., #400, Washington, DC 20001.

Council for Exceptional Children, 1920 Association Dr., Reston, VA 22091.

Disability Rights Education & Defense Fund, Inc., 1616 P St., #100, Washington, DC 20036.

Education Law Center, 155 Washington St., #209, Newark, NJ 07102.

Information Center for Handicapped Children, 605 G St., N.W., Philadelphia, PA 19102.

Jerome N. Frank Legal Services Organization, Yale Law School, Box 401-A Yale Station, New Haven, CT 06520.

Parent Educational Advocacy Training Center, 228 S. Pitt St., #300, Alexandria, VA 22314.

Public Interest Law Center, 125 S. 9th St., #700, Philadelphia, PA 19107.

References

Burpee v. *Manchester School District*, 661 F. Supp. 731 (D NH 1987).

Michael F. v. *Cambridge School Department* (D MA 1987).

Rollison v. *Biggs*, 660 F. Supp. 875 (D DE 1987).

Rowley v. *Board of Education of the Hendrick Hudson Center School District*, 102 S. Ct. 3034 (1982).

THEODORE A. SUSSAN *is an attorney who limits his practice to special education; he has offices in Spotswood, Middlesex County, New Jersey.*

*For serious chronic biological disorders in children and adolescents,
the focus of nonpharmacological therapy by health care
professionals should be on supportive caring.*

Professional Supportive Caring for Children and Adolescents with Chronic Neurobiological Disorders

Kris A. McLoughlin

For serious chronic biological disorders in children and adolescents like diabetes or neurobiological disorders (NBD) such as autism and pervasive developmental disorders, bipolar and major depressive disorders, schizophrenia, Tourette's syndrome, obsessive-compulsive disorder, anxiety disorders, and attention deficit hyperactivity disorder, the focus of nonpharmacological treatment by health care professionals—physicians, nurses, social workers, and psychologists—should be on supportive caring. Health care professionals should help afflicted children reach their maximum potential and gain an understanding of how the biological disorder may affect their lives. Health care professionals should also help families cope with the ongoing stress and grief present when a family member has a serious chronic disorder. Parents are never blamed when their child has a brain tumor or a seizure disorder. In the same way, parents should not be blamed if their child has an NBD.

Working with the Children

For many children with NBD, pharmacological therapy may be very helpful (see Part One). Such therapy can often mean the difference between a child's psychosis and a child's ability to function in many social and intellectual interactions. Therefore, it is essential that children with NBD have physicians who are expert in using the most modern neuropharmacological medications. In addition, because the NBD affects children's emotions, behavior, and cognition, an intense program with both psychological and educational components is needed to help them realize their optimal functioning.

Treating children with an NBD or any other serious, chronic disorder is a complex, potentially daunting task. At times, the task will appear overwhelming because of the disorder's chronicity and the often perplexing, difficult-to-manage symptoms. Along with providing appropriate pharmacological therapy, the treatment program should try to (1) help the children develop a positive sense of self, (2) nurture their attempts to build constructive relationships with others, and (3) maximize their strengths so that they can lead as fulfilling lives as possible, despite their handicaps.

To understand children's struggles with their illness, health care professionals must connect with and relate to them. An excellent way to do this is to spend some time in their home setting. Developing a relationship with children who have NBD and who perceive reality inconsistently can be a long and confusing process. I always keep in mind how scary and confusing relationships must be for them. And I begin by exploring what is special about each child. Understanding a person's deficits is important for treatment, but it does not build relationships. Trying to grasp the children's strengths—for example, the things they appreciate and want to learn about or develop—not only helps me understand them as people but also gives me an idea of their potential. It helps to recall children's strengths when they are going through an acute crisis, too. When they are losing control, I have often found that I can most easily contain or deescalate them by trying to connect back to one of their strengths or interests. Children develop a greater sense of security when they realize that another person knows them well enough, even when they are out of control, to refer to their strengths and interests with familiar words.

To help children with NBD form a positive sense of self, health professionals must teach these children to separate their behaviors from themselves as human beings. This must be done frequently and consistently so that children with NBD begin to understand that they are not "bad" people, but rather that some of their actions (behaviors) may be embarrassing or harmful. This approach is particularly important when these children grow older and begin to recognize that some of their behaviors are "crazy," producing feelings of guilt, sadness, anger, and confusion. When the professional-child relationship is strong enough, children with NBD are able to use the health professional for support as well as for reality testing. This helps the children grieve their sense of loss and isolation while yet maintaining a sense of self.

Caring for children with NBD involves assisting them with developmental struggles and life events. They often cannot distinguish between a struggle secondary to their brain disorder and a common human struggle. It is important to help them acquire problem-solving skills, plus social and interactive skills. Because many children with NBD have difficulties expressing themselves appropriately, it is hard for them to get their needs met. Giving them the tools to communicate more effectively can help them alter ineffective patterns of interaction and allow them to understand and work better within the framework of their expressive deficits.

When caring for children with NBD, it is important to share a part of yourself with them. They need to see you as a human being who is trying to make a connection. I have found that when children and adolescents have shared a positive experience with me, they begin to see how they can have a positive impact on others.

Working with the Families

Wolraich (1989) states that one of the physician's most important jobs in caring for a child with mental retardation is communicating with the child's family. He recommends that when parents first learn about their child's diagnosis, the physician should focus on the parents' reactions to the diagnosis. Because parents often wonder what they did wrong and may feel guilty, they should be told honestly and clearly about their child's brain disorder. The physician should explicitly state that it is *not* the parents' fault. Parents should also be told that the diagnosis implies a significant loss, and that it is normal to grieve such a loss (Wolraich, 1989).

In my experience, a similar approach is often used with parents of a child diagnosed with spina bifida, muscular dystrophy, or other chronic illnesses. The physician may discuss progress in medical research and hope for new treatments, but the focus of the initial conference is on the reality of how the child's serious disorder will permanently affect the child and the family. The same caring approach should also be used for families when a child is initially diagnosed with an NBD. At the same time, the process of the family's grieving must be addressed, too.

Previous clinical studies had formulated a theory of "time-bound" grief characterized by specific stages of shock, despair, guilt, withdrawal, acceptance, and adjustment. Based on this theory, the focus of much of medicine and psychiatry has been to help the family "resolve" their grief. However, when Wikler, Wasow, and Hatfield (1981) explored chronic grief among parents whose children had mental retardation, they described their grief as an *ongoing* process: parents talked about numerous occasions when intense feelings of grieving were reevoked and experienced. Likewise, chronic grieving best describes the reactions of families whose children have a serious chronic NBD. In my experience with such families, it is not uncommon to see feelings of guilt, anger, despair, and shock emerge, subside, and reemerge. Professionals should understand and accept this ongoing process, and they should help the family cope with both the erratic course of the child's illness and the waxing-and-waning nature of the family's grief.

Families whose children have NBD can use supportive, reality-based counseling (Bernheim, 1982). They do not need "therapy" any more than a family whose child has any other severe chronic illness like cystic fibrosis does. Goals for supportive family counseling should include the following: (1) Give the family a good understanding of the biological nature of the child's illness. (2) Facilitate parental and sibling coping with the persistent stress of living with a chronically disabled child. (3) Teach the family problem-solving approaches that reduce stress. (4) Help parents develop the skills necessary to teach their child with an NBD how to manage his or her problems better. (5) Educate the family about the availability—or lack of—educational, social, vocational, respite, and legal services in the community.

A parent-professional partnership can be beneficial to the disabled child. Koegel and others (1982) found that training mothers to be cotherapists or teachers of their autistic children was more effective than a therapist's direct instruction to the child. Doane, Goldstein, Mikowitz, and Falloon (1986) confirmed that parental involvement had a significant positive effect in families caring for a member with schizophrenia. The relapse rate was reduced in patients whose families were taught constructive problem-solving techniques to handle stressful situations, compared to families who were not taught specific problem-solving techniques. Treatment goals should be formulated by parents and professionals as *equal* partners. All interventions should be reevaluated regularly with the family. By recognizing that parents know more about their child than anybody else does, the health professional becomes a caring partner with the parents, rather than the sole expert (Bristol and Schopler, 1989).

In most cases, the family is the child's *major* source of support. But the family must also be supported. I have found that families gain a tremendous amount of support from groups such as the National Alliance for the Mentally Ill Children and Adolescents Network (NAMI CAN). Such groups provide access to important information regarding educational programs, government funding, legislation, and clinical advances in the field. Many families are unaware that resources such as NAMI CAN exist. Health professionals should routinely refer families to such resources.

As scientific knowledge progresses, there is hope that better treatments, and possibly cures, can be found for all NBD. While health care professionals should always nurture a sense of hope in the child and family, they should also acknowledge the limitations of modern medical practice. Our treatment must focus on caring, because a cure is not yet possible. It is only with this focus that the true needs of the child and the caring family can be met.

References

Bernheim, K. F. "Supportive Family Counseling." *Schizophrenia Bulletin*, 1982, *8* (4), 634–640.
Bristol, M., and Schopler, E. "The Family in the Treatment of Autism." In *Treatments of*

Psychiatric Disorders: A Task Force Report of the American Psychiatric Association. Vol. 1. Washington, D.C.: American Psychiatric Association, 1989.

Doane, J. A., Goldstein, D. J., Mikowitz, D. J., and Falloon, I. R. "The Impact of Individual and Family Treatment on the Affective Climate of Families of Schizophrenics." *British Journal of Psychiatry,* 1986, *148,* 279-287.

Koegel, R. L., Schreibman, L., Britten, K. R., Burke, J. C., and O'Neill, R. E. "A Comparison of Parent Training to Direct Child Treatment." In R. L. Koegel, A. Rincover, and A. L. Egel (eds.), *Educating and Understanding Autistic Children.* San Diego, Calif.: College-Hill Press, 1982.

Wikler, L., Wasow, M., and Hatfield, E. "Chronic Sorrow Revisited: Parent Versus Professional Depiction of the Adjustment of Parents of Mentally Retarded Children." *American Journal of Orthopsychiatry,* 1981, *51* (1), 63-70.

Wolraich, M. "Counseling Families of Children with Mental Retardation." In *Treatments of Psychiatric Disorders: A Task Force Report of the American Psychiatric Association.* Vol. 1. Washington, D.C.: American Psychiatric Association, 1989.

KRIS A. MCLOUGHLIN, a psychiatric clinical nurse specialist, has a private practice in Boston and is a clinical instructor in psychiatry at Tufts University School of Medicine.

CONCLUDING REMARKS

The chapters in Part One, written by some of our country's leading neuroscience researchers, report the scientific findings from neurobiology through 1991. They document that many serious chronic "psychiatric" disorders in children and adolescents are, in fact, physical disorders—neurobiological disorders (NBD)—characterized by malfunctions or malformations of the brain or both. Among these physical disorders are autism and pervasive developmental disorders, obsessive-compulsive disorder, Tourette's syndrome, bipolar and major depressive disorders, attention deficit hyperactivity disorder, anxiety disorders, and schizophrenia. In addition, the chapters with scientific data relevant to conduct disorder enable us to see that, as neuroscience progresses, other disorders may be filtered out into various new categories, based on neurobiological findings. It is very likely that, as our knowledge about NBD expands and changes, other diagnoses will be added to the current list of NBD. This volume documents that we are at last on the right track: the road of reproducible scientific data, empirical evidence, and scientifically documented efficacy.

Starting from the scientific evidence that NBD are physical disorders, the chapters in Part Two highlight ways in which our society needs to integrate the neuroscience revolution into daily practice. Based on the irrefutable findings of the neuroscience revolution, it is not acceptable to deny the importance of the etiology of a child's aberrant behavior, emotions, or cognitive reactions. To really help a person with an NBD, it is essential to begin with an accurate diagnosis, based on the most current neuroscientific data.

In a larger sense, this volume in the New Directions for Mental Health Services series points to the need for a continuum of services and supports for children and adolescents severely disabled with neurobiological disorders. Now is the time for our country to create a continuum of medical, educational, vocational, social, domiciliary, and rehabilitation services to meet the needs of human beings of all ages severely disabled by these often devastating chronic physical illnesses. Those would be New Directions indeed. And in deed.

Enid Peschel
Richard Peschel
Carol W. Howe
James W. Howe
Editors

ENID PESCHEL is co-director of the Program for Humanities in Medicine and assistant professor (adjunct) of internal medicine at Yale University School of Medicine.

RICHARD PESCHEL is professor of therapeutic radiology at Yale University School of Medicine.

CAROL W. HOWE is membership chair of the National Alliance for the Mentally Ill Children and Adolescents Network (NAMI CAN) Advisory Council, Arlington, Virginia.

JAMES W. HOWE, an economist, was president of the National Alliance for the Mentally Ill (NAMI), Arlington, Virginia, from 1984 to 1986.

Name Index

Akshoomoff, N. A., 21, 22
Alvir, J., 81
Amaya-Jackson, L., 2, 45, 50
Ambrosini, P. J., 43, 44
Amsel, R., 52, 57
Anders, T. F., 15, 16
Anderson, L., 56, 62
Andreasen, N. C., 95
Andrulonis, P. A., 51, 56
Arin, D. M., 20, 22
Arnold, L. E., 60, 62
Asarnow, R. F., 16, 75
Ashtari, M., 81
Asnis, L., 44
Astill, J. L., 55, 56

Barker, P., 60, 62
Barkley, R. A., 50
Bartak, L., 16
Bauer, L., 28
Bauman, M. L., 20, 22
Behar, D., 57
Beitchman, J. H., 75
Bemporad, J. R., 53, 56
Benkelfat, C., 85, 86
Bennett, W. G., 56, 62
Berman, K. F., 80, 82
Bernheim, K. F., 126
Best, A. M., 114, 116
Bianca, J., 44
Biederman, J., 51, 56
Bilder, R. M., 81
Black, B., 2, 65, 70
Bogerts, B., 80, 81
Bonagura, N., 52, 57, 62
Boppana, V., 61, 63
Bott, L., 75
Boyd, J. H., 104
Boyle, M. H., 60, 62
Brady, J., 104
Brent, D. A., 2, 39, 44, 53, 56
Bridger, W. H., 57
Bridges, C. I., 61, 63
Bristol, M., 126
Britten, K. R., 127
Brown, G. L., 54, 56, 57, 87
Brown, R. V., 53, 56

Brunn, R. D., 33
Bukstein, O., 53, 56
Burchard, J. D., 97, 100
Burke, J. C., 127
Burke, J. D., 104
Burroughs, J., 38
Byles, J. A., 62

Cadman, D. T., 62
Cahill, J., 104
Campbell, M., 15, 55, 56, 61, 62, 75
Cantwell, D. P., 2, 45, 50
Casanova, M. F., 82
Catlin, J. A., 62
Chambers, W. J., 43, 44
Char, W. F., 70
Cheslow, D., 87
Chess, S., 15
Christison, G. W., 82
Ciaranello, A. L., 83, 86
Ciaranello, R. D., 1, 9, 15, 16, 17, 83, 86
Cichetti, D., 53, 56
Clanon, T. L., 63
Clarke, R. T., 97, 100
Clayton, P. J., 38
Coccaro, E. F., 2, 51, 54, 55, 56, 57
Cochrane, K., 56
Coffey, M., 87
Cohen, D., 33
Cohen, R., 114, 116
Cohen, R. M., 50, 57, 86, 87
Colner, G., 62
Combrinck-Graham, L., 70
Comings, D. E., 33
Conners, C. K., 60, 62, 63
Cooper, T. B., 56
Courchesne, E., 1, 16, 19, 20, 21, 22, 23, 80, 82
Crawford, J. M., 62
Cunningham, M. A., 60, 62

Davies, M., 43, 44
Davies, S., 44
Davis, K. L., 56
De Long, R., 22
Degreef, G., 81
DeLisi, L. E., 82

SUBJECT INDEX

ORDERING INFORMATION

NEW DIRECTIONS FOR MENTAL HEALTH SERVICES is a series of paperback books that presents timely and readable volumes on subjects of concern to clinicians, administrators, and others involved in the care of the mentally disabled. Each volume is devoted to one topic and includes a broad range of authoritative articles written by noted specialists in the field. Books in the series are published quarterly in Fall, Winter, Spring, and Summer and are available for purchase by subscription as well as by single copy.

SUBSCRIPTIONS for 1992 cost $52.00 for individuals (a savings of 20 percent over single-copy prices) and $70.00 for institutions, agencies, and libraries. Please do not send institutional checks for personal subscriptions. Standing orders are accepted.

SINGLE COPIES cost $17.95 when payment accompanies order. (California, New Jersey, New York, and Washington, D.C., residents please include appropriate sales tax.) Billed orders will be charged postage and handling.

DISCOUNTS FOR QUANTITY ORDERS are available. Please write to the address below for information.

ALL ORDERS must include either the name of an individual or an official purchase order number. Please submit your order as follows:
    Subscriptions: specify series and year subscription is to begin
    Single copies: include individual title code (such as MHS1)

MAIL ALL ORDERS TO:
    Jossey-Bass Publishers
    350 Sansome Street
    San Francisco, California 94104

FOR SALES OUTSIDE OF THE UNITED STATES CONTACT:
    Maxwell Macmillan International Publishing Group
    866 Third Avenue
    New York, New York 10022